"No aspect of postmodern life is more broken than.... 5
brings more wholeness to broken sexuality than the gospel of Jesus Christ. No ministry is more helpful in applying the grace of the cross and the empty tomb to broken sexuality than Harvest USA."

Dr. Phil Ryken, President, Wheaton College

"'Line upon line and precept upon precept,' (Isaiah 28:10, 13) is the searchingly fresh approach David White has taken in writing both the book and the accompanying *Leader's Guide*. Rather than highlighting a representative collection of truths applicable to this life and death struggle for sexual sanity, David White seeks to build, from foundation to roof, a theologically thorough and helpfully profound approach to this dimension of fighting the good fight in the Christian life. He has given me, and I trust all who read and work through this material, substantive help. Thank you, David."

Joseph V. Novenson, Senior Teaching Pastor, Lookout Mountain Presbyterian Church, TN

"Here is what you get in *Sexual Sanity for Men*: Scripture, connecting to real life, given in daily portions (not too much, not too little) from a friend who is open, honest, understands the struggle, and has actually grown in these matters. That means he wrote a guide that you will find very helpful *and* he listens to these words himself every day. It is a great book for all men, especially those who are teetering on hopelessness."

Edward T. Welch, PhD, faculty member CCEF; psychologist; author of *Shame Interrupted*

"Harvest USA is a time-tested ministry that changes lives with the gospel. They know how to speak the truth into your life with gentleness and love. Their skills and expertise have never been more needed by the church. Support it and become involved."

Dr. Timothy Keller, Senior Pastor, Redeemer Presbyterian Church, New York, NY and author of *The Reason for God*

"It's about time somebody said it and said it this way! This is a book that will transform a very difficult and painful subject into a walk of faith and faithfulness that will bring joy, release, and praise. Not only that, the *Leader's Guide* is incredibly helpful, practical, and profound. Give this (and the *Leader's Guide*) to every guy you know, even if you have to wrap it in a plain, brown paper wrapper. They will 'rise up and call you blessed.'"

Steve Brown, Key Life radio broadcaster; author of *Three Free Sins: God Isn't Mad at You*

"I know of no resource that is written to help men who are struggling with sexual sin that is more soundly biblical, drenched with the gospel, and practical at the street level. I am thankful that this resource now exists and will recommend it again and again. Here is a welcome for men to come out of the hiding, to embrace that there is nothing that could be revealed about them that hasn't already been covered by the blood of Jesus, and to believe that God has given them every grace that they need to fight the battle with sexual sin."

Paul David Tripp, President, Paul Tripp Ministries; best-selling author

SEXUAL SANITY FOR MEN
RE-CREATING YOUR MIND
IN A CRAZY CULTURE

David White

New
Growth
Press
www.newgrowthpress.com

New Growth Press, Greensboro, NC 27404
Copyright ©2012 by Harvest USA.

Unless otherwise indicated, all Scripture quotations are from The *Holy Bible, English
Standard Version*® (ESV®), copyright © 2001 by Crossway, a publishing ministry of
Good News Publishers. Used by permission. All rights reserved.

Scripture quotations marked NIV are from the *Holy Bible: New International Version*®.
(NIV®). Copyright ©1973, 1978, 1984 by International Bible Society. Used by
permission of Zondervan Publishing House. All rights reserved.

Cover Design: Faceout Books, faceoutbooks.com
Interior Design and Typesetting: Lisa Parnell, lparnell.com

ISBN 978-1-936768-99-8

Library of Congress Cataloging-in-Publication Data
White, David, 1970–
   Sexual sanity for men : re-creating your mind in a crazy culture / David White.
      p. cm.
   Includes bibliographical references and index.
   ISBN 978-1-936768-99-8 (alk. paper)
   1. Sex—Religious aspects—Christianity. 2. Men—Sexual behavior. 3. Men—
Religious life. I. Title.
   BT708.W43 2012
   248.8'42—dc23
                                                                                    2012027982

Printed in Canada

19 18 17 16 15 14 13 12   1 2 3 4 5

CONTENTS

In loving memory of Sandra Jo White

October 26, 1966–October 9, 2009

God used our marriage to teach me what it means to love.

ACKNOWLEDGMENTS

I am extremely grateful to have the two most patient bosses in the world, John Freeman and Nicholas Black. I was deeply blessed by their understanding of the challenges of single parenting, walking through grief, and juggling day-to-day ministry responsibilities while trying to get this project done. Thank you, brothers, for believing in me and gently pushing this to completion.

Harvest USA is grateful for New Growth's partnership with a relatively unknown ministry, and I personally thank Barbara Juliani for your patience with this novice writer.

This book wouldn't exist apart from my colleague, Dan Wilson, who brainstormed this material with me and helped shape the structure. The best material in Section 2 was shamelessly stolen from you.

I praise God for the incredible support of my staff team: John, Nicholas, Ed, Irene, Scott, Ward, Ellen, and Bob. You have laughed and cried with me and consistently point me to the hope we have in Jesus. You are family—serving together is a wonderful foretaste of life in the kingdom.

My extended family (on both sides) has been a great source of comfort and healing in the midst of heartache. I praise God for his sweet restorative work in all our lives and look forward to what is yet in store.

There have been literally hundreds of people praying for me and my girls through this season, many of whom I've never even met. Your prayers have enabled me to persevere through the hardest trial of my life with a peace and joy I would not have thought possible.

I minister to the most courageous men I know. They are willing to face the pain of their pasts, be exposed at their worst in the present, and seek Christ in the midst of it all. Your willingness to allow me to hear your stories and be a part of this journey is an incredible honor. Thank you.

Jim Bergwall, your friendship is the most unexpected blessing to come from my loss. I praise God for your willingness to share life with me and to teach me to pray as I never have before.

Charis and Sydney, you are the sweetest blessings in my life. Being your dad has taught me more about God's heart than anything else I've experienced. I'm grateful to still have so much of Mommy because I have you!

Finally, Jennifer, I am blown away by God's sweet gift of you. More than I could have imagined. A bright, shining light after a long period of deep darkness. I am thrilled you are the wife he set apart for me and I can't wait to see the plans he has for us!

INTRODUCTION

George sat in church, unable to focus on the sermon. He was a mess. The night before, he had encouraged his wife to go to bed without him because "the game wouldn't be over until *really* late."

The truth was, he'd been looking forward all day to checking out some porn sites. While mowing the grass that Saturday morning, he had thought his plan through. Now, sitting in church, he felt the guilt and shame. He felt miserable, exhausted from being up so late—he had lost track of time and didn't go to bed until after 2 a.m. He's ready to doze off in the middle of the sermon. He was harsh and irritable with his family all morning, resulting in a tense, silent drive to church.

On one level, he hates what he's done. He looks around and wonders what people would say if they knew, especially since he's a deacon. He can't imagine telling his friends—let alone his wife. But even in the midst of his guilt, he knows he enjoyed it. The images continue to swirl in his mind, and he can't wait to go back. He gets a thrill from porn like nothing else in his life. He could laugh out loud as he compares sitting and listening to a sermon with the adventure and pleasure of the night before. He hates it and he loves it at the same time.

George has been a Christian for a long time and knows how God says he *should* live. And he wants to live for God, to be a loving husband and father. But the pull of his lust is strong, and he can't imagine his life without it.

Do you know what it's like to sit in church, feeling guilty? Are there behaviors in your life that fill you with shame? Are you living in the tension of doing things you know to be wrong while being incapable of imagining your life without them?

Sexual sin is a *huge* problem in the body of Christ. If you're struggling with sexual sin, you need to know that *you are not alone in the church.* Age and doctrinal distinctions don't matter when it comes to this issue. Sexual sin is an equal opportunity pathogen of the soul. Men (and women) of every generation and theological bent have been impacted by our decadent culture and the lusts of their hearts. There are pastors going to strip clubs while away at conferences; deacons looking at online teen porn; elders struggling in silence with same-sex attraction, looking at gay porn and having anonymous encounters with men; Sunday school teachers hiring prostitutes and having affairs with unbelieving coworkers. Sexual sin is radically impacting the church, from the man in the pulpit to the unbelieving visitor in the pew, to everyone in between.

Here's the bottom line: You need this book because all of us have a sexuality that has been impacted by the fall and which desperately needs redemption. All sexuality is broken, on some level. None of us go through life with blinders on until we meet that perfect someone of the opposite sex and then live the rest of our lives with eyes only for her, faithfully dedicated to focusing all of our delight and passion on her. None of us live that way, *naturally.* If you're honest, you admit that you struggle with lust in some way. All of us have a sexuality that requires radical *supernatural* intervention! We are all sexual beings in the process of redemption. Therefore, we need to take this area of Christian living seriously.

The other reason you need this book is that sexual sin has the power to utterly destroy your life. I have seen men throw away their families, shipwreck their careers, end up in financial ruin, even land in prison, because of sexual sin. Although their outward behaviors may be very different, all of these men have something in common: At one time they believed they had it all under control. What's even more troubling: Some of them believe they *still* have things under control! We'll talk about this more in Week 1, but for now suffice it to say that sin in general—and sexual sin in particular—is profoundly deceiving. Men destroy their lives because they're utterly blinded by the pleasure of sin and are willing to sacrifice everything rather than lose what feels like life to them.

Every man wrestles with a sexuality in need of redemption. And with sexual sin, the stakes are as high as they can possibly be: marriage, family, friendships, finances, career . . . most significantly, our *faith* is at stake! As we'll discover, sex is about worship, so our rebellion in this area speaks volumes about the depth, maybe even the reality, of our faith.

You are not reading this book by accident. Our sovereign God has, by some means, placed it in your hands, because it's time to deal with these issues in your life. He wants to take you deeper. Nevertheless, no matter how diligent you are, please realize at the outset that you will *never* be free from the battle in this life. I pray that by God's grace you will experience greater freedom from sexual sin than you ever thought possible, but you must be committed to staying in the battle for life. Freedom is not total deliverance from temptation, which is what we wish it would be. Freedom is the increasing ability to choose holiness out of love for Christ, *despite* the relentlessness of temptation! This is the hard truth, but the blessing is that we receive more of Christ as we are committed to the fight!

And this battle is profoundly spiritual. The enemy is deeply invested in keeping us enslaved and ineffective for the kingdom of God. Men often say that temptation gets worse once they begin to attack this issue intentionally. As hard as that is, it's a good sign!

Know this—doing this hard work represents significant growth in your masculinity. No reader is the same: you may be a slacker who has never applied himself to anything, or the CEO of a Fortune 500 company whose entire life has been a strenuous climb to the top. The hard work I have in view has nothing to do with your work ethic. Whether you're an underachiever, overachiever, or someone in between, we all naturally shrink back from the challenge of staring our sin in the face and sincerely owning the worst truths about ourselves. The sad reality is, even as Christians who profess our need of forgiveness in Christ, we resist being *truly known* by others. Rather than being exposed in our weakness, we try desperately to make change alone.

God is calling you out of hiding. He is calling you to face who you are and risk letting others know the man you are trying to conceal. He is calling you to stop squandering your life on short-term, guilty pleasures in order to experience a life of deeper pleasure and joy. Are you ready for the challenge?

THE GENERAL THEMES OF THIS BOOK

At its core, our sexual insanity is idolatry. Like the Israelites who were brought out of slavery in Egypt into the Promised Land, but whose later idolatry and rebellion resulted in pagan capture and exile in Babylon, so our sin also keeps us in chains, living a joyless and often fruitless "Christian" life. Many of us came to faith with great joy and experienced wondrous freedom over past sexual sin, only to have it slowly creep back and consume us. It's as if we too entered the Promised Land, but eventually ended up in spiritual exile. This existence falls woefully short of the promises offered to us in the Scriptures. So, we will begin by examining the truth about our sexual sin and its effect on our lives, both physically and spiritually.

We will then move on to examine the work of Christ. Too often the Christian life is seen as "you get to go to heaven when you die," as if the death and resurrection of Jesus hold no relevance or power for *today.* This could not be further from the truth! The heart of the gospel is that the kingdom of God came into the world. In a word, this is *re-creation*, overturning the effects of the curse of the fall and restoring *shalom* to the world. In Hebrew, *shalom* means peace, not simply in the sense of an absence of conflict, but rather a broad, overarching wholeness and restoration. It refers to a world that is "full of the knowledge of the LORD as the waters cover the sea" and where "justice roll[s] down like waters, and righteousness like an ever-flowing stream" (Isaiah 11:9; Amos 5:24).

This restorative work is why the Bible declares that those who are in Christ are a new creation (2 Corinthians 5:17). Although this will always be incomplete until Christ's return, it is nevertheless true. Christ died to redeem us from our sin and to establish his kingdom in our hearts and through us to the rest of creation. In this way, Christ's work of atonement is the reestablishing of the Father's mandate at the time of creation, to subdue the earth for the glory of our King, the new Adam. All this is to say, the gospel meets us in the here and now, empowering transformation where we live *today.* The true Christian life couldn't be further from the pie-in-the-sky-when-you-die approach of too many Christians!

Finally, we'll consider the practical implications of this rich theology and how it applies to your struggle with sexual sin. We'll spend time investigating how our union with Christ relates to the change process. We'll uncover the radical way the Bible says we're supposed to do church, and how the community of faith is crucial to personal transformation. And, of course, we'll examine the call to personal transformation, which always includes accountability and resisting sinful behaviors, but is actually so much more. God does not call us to a place of "absent sin," but radical life transformation. He is calling us to be conformed to the image of Jesus, which means rediscovering what it truly means to be a man and to experience the wonder of that life breaking into our current existence.

We have trouble getting our minds around this reality: The Bible seems to suggest there will be *no sex for all eternity*![1] Sex points beyond itself to something better. Brother, an orgasm is a fleeting glimpse and foretaste of an infinitely greater, *eternal* pleasure that is beyond our ability even to imagine.

My prayer is that through this book you will discover the wonder of a redeemed sexuality, restored to the pure joy and guiltless pleasure of God's design, but even more, as Paul prayed for the Ephesians, "that according to the riches of his glory he may grant you to be strengthened with power through his Spirit in your inner being, so that Christ may dwell in your hearts through faith—that you, being rooted and grounded in love, may have strength to comprehend with all the saints what is the breadth and length and height and depth, and to know the love of Christ that surpasses knowledge, that you may be filled with all the fullness of God" (Ephesians 3:16–19). May we have eyes to see by faith the infinite joy offered to us and stop selling our birthright for a bowl of soup![2]

HOW TO USE THIS BOOK

The most important thing to remember as you use this book is: You are *not alone*! I hope you'll use this book in the context of community: with a mentor, or in a small men's group. If you don't have anyone at the moment, get started, but please commit to praying for God's provision of Christian brothers to help you process the material. One of the underlying themes of this book is that the Christian life was never intended to be lived in isolation.

Further, know that there are no easy fixes. Your growth out of sexual sin requires work and intentionality. Passively reading this book is not a "magic hammer" that will easily smash your struggle with sin and restore your sexual sanity. You must commit to working through the questions, taking time to reflect honestly, and facing the hard facts about yourself. Little change will come from this book if you do not actively seek to apply its teachings *personally*. The "For Reflection" sections in each chapter are designed to help you bring the teaching down to ground level, where you live.

Each chapter, or week, has been divided into five daily readings. The goal is for you to spend time regularly focusing on this issue. As you read through the material daily, meditate on the Scripture, and prayerfully work through the questions, you'll stay aware of these issues in your life and grow in understanding the inner workings of your heart.

SECTION 1:
LIFE IN EXILE

WEEK 1:
LIFE IN THE WASTELAND

KEY CONCEPT: Sexual sin brings desolation. It promises excitement and pleasure, but delivers discontent and insatiable craving, often bringing ruin to God's blessings: family, friendships, vocation, and health. It leads to an insane life. What seems like a purely personal sin is always relationally destructive. In our guilt we isolate ourselves or lash out in anger. We compound our sin as we manipulate and lie to cover our tracks. While culture tells us that sexual sin is a sign of our strength, we know the stark contrast between our fantasy life and our struggles to cope with the real world. As Christians, our sin drives us into hiding, and we begin to live wearing a mask. The disconnect between our private life and public façade perpetuates our insecurity.

But there is hope! There is a Deliverer who breaks into this downward spiral, empowering us to face life's challenges with confidence, and replacing our gnawing desires and despair with joy and contentment.

DAY 1: THE CONSEQUENCES OF SEXUAL SIN

Do you know the experience of slavery? Do you know what it's like to want to stop masturbating, looking at porn, or having anonymous sex, and realizing that you *can't*? You've made hundreds of promises to God and others, but your words increasingly ring hollow—even to yourself. You've tried for years to change, without success, so you know eventually you'll be at it again . . .

Worse, have you suffered from seemingly uncontrollable thoughts? You try to restrain them, but they keep drifting back to certain memories, individuals, or fantasies. They break in constantly, causing distraction. You've tried to pray, fast, memorize Scripture, but nothing seems to work for very long. The thoughts, desires, and attractions come back, leaving you feeling defeated and hopeless. You lose hope that victory over your thoughts is possible.

How has your struggle with sexual sin—in your desires and behavior—impacted your life? It appears so innocuous at first. Perhaps masturbation is a guilty pleasure, but it seems relatively harmless. Using porn or fantasy to fuel your behavior is an obvious necessity. But there is always progression. What starts with swimsuit ads turns into soft porn. Then you want to see more and more. Eventually pictures aren't enough, and the Internet makes video downloads so easy. What began as a pleasant escape from the humdrum routine or pressures of life becomes an obsession. Some men spend hours every day surfing the Internet for new porn. Others pursue connection through chat rooms or phone sex. Many end up doing what they previously thought impossible—seeking out sexual encounters.

This increasing escalation has a price tag. We all have a very finite life, and yet every day men are sacrificing things of infinite value to pursue their sexual desires. The time, energy, and money invested in pursuing sexual sin robs from your family, your future security, your career aspirations, your ability to serve God and others. Even our health becomes a casualty. HIV and other STDs abound. The strain of living a double life results in depression, ulcers, and anxiety.

In Psalm 32, David describes the cost of hidden sin, "For when I kept silent, my bones wasted away through my groaning all day long. For day and night your hand was heavy upon me; my strength was dried up as by the heat of summer" (Psalm 32:3–4). We willingly sacrifice everything most dear to us—spouse, children, career, financial success, even our faith—on the altar of our sexual desires. What has your sin cost you? Are you ready to be restored to sexual sanity?

Even if your struggle hasn't escalated to the degree just described, have you noticed that your desires are taking up more space in your head? Maybe you're able to manage your behavior on a day-to-day basis, but do you invest time carefully planning your next opportunity? Or relishing the memories of your last exploit? How do you respond to others when your carefully orchestrated plan is thwarted? Maybe your behavior looks okay on the outside, but inwardly you're enslaved.

You're not alone in this battle. Every Christian who wants to grow in holiness needs to face the fact that there are places in his life where he is still enslaved by sin.

Paul poignantly describes the experience of every Christian battling against sin:

> I do not understand my own actions. For I do not do what I want, but I do the very thing I hate. Now if I do what I do not want, I agree with the law, that it is good. So now it is no longer I who do it, but sin that dwells within me. For I know that nothing good dwells in me, that is, in my flesh. For I have the desire to do what is right, but not the ability to carry it out. For I do not do the good I want, but the evil I do not want is what I keep on doing. Now if I do what I do not want, it is no longer I who do it, but sin that dwells within me.
>
> So I find it to be a law that when I want to do right, evil lies close at hand. For I delight in the law of God, in my inner being, but I see in my members another law waging war against the law of my mind and making me captive to the law of sin that dwells in my members. Wretched man that I am! Who will deliver me from this body of death? Thanks be to God through Jesus Christ our Lord! So then, I myself serve the law of God with my mind, but with my flesh I serve the law of sin. (Romans 7:15–25)

There is a profound sense of slavery and frustration in our inability to overcome our struggle with sin. You can almost see Paul beating his head against the wall in utter exasperation. And the battle is on two fronts. We continue in sin we hate, and at the same time woefully neglect God's calling to love him and others.

Brother, your situation is not unique—it was experienced by the most prolific writer of the New Testament, the eminent apostle who fearlessly took the message of Christ to Rome, the place of ultimate power and opposition to Jesus in the first century. And it has been the experience of every other leader in the church since and every man in the pew! All of us continue to struggle significantly with sin as Christians and sexual sin in particular reduces us to slavery.

For Reflection:

1. Describe the pain sexual sin has caused in your life. What does it feel like to be a slave of a behavior or desires? How has it affected your behavior around others?

2. What has sexual sin "cost" you? Be specific.

3. What "encouragement" can you gain from Paul's struggle with sin in Romans 7?

DAY 2: THE REALITY OF GUILT

Do you know the experience of guilt? Sometimes it's acute—a stabbing pain in your gut. At other times, it's a dull, gnawing in your soul; you feel a vague sense of wrongness about life, and when you stop to focus on why, the memory of your sin floods back. You long to be free from guilt, but as your failure persists, the pain continues.

As a Christian, the guilt you experience over your sin is unavoidable. You know the truth. You know how God has called you to live. You know what you should be doing, and what you shouldn't. (In some sense, be encouraged by the presence of guilt. It can be evidence of the Spirit's work, convicting your heart.)

Further, our experience of guilt is compounded because sexual sin is always clustered with other sins. Lies and deceit are the constant companions of sexual sin. We squander time and resources, neglecting our calling as husband, father, son, employee, church member. Sometimes we steal to support our behaviors. All these things deepen the reality of our guilt.

Because we keep our sin hidden, our guilt surfaces in other ways, and impacts our relationships with others. We're irritable and impatient. We become withdrawn and sullen. Sometimes we rage, even scaring ourselves. Even if you manage to hide your behavior for decades, there is always fallout from sin. Sin always infects our relationships with both God and others. Spending the evening looking at porn online will impact who you are at work the next day—for instance, how well you're able to function and interact with others, especially female coworkers. When you stop at the adult bookstore (or bathhouse, etc.) on the way home from work, it affects who you are at the dinner table with your family. When you've spent time at work having a sexual chat online, you're a different man at the home Bible study that night. If you're having suggestive conversations with a coworker, it will affect how you interact with your wife once the kids are in bed. You may be able to hide your sexual sin, but there are always relational consequences.

One more thing: A greater ability to mask these things—to compartmentalize and hide the effects of your guilt—is not an indication of your strength. It doesn't demonstrate how much smarter you are than anyone else. Quite the opposite— it actually shows that you are in grave danger!

Proverbs 26:12 warns, "Do you see a man who is wise in his own eyes? There is more hope for a fool than for him." This is a stinging indictment. Believing that we can pull the wool over the eyes of others puts us in a worse position than a fool. Further, the book of Galatians, written so we would learn to rest in God's mercy through Christ rather than our own good works, nevertheless warns, "Do not be deceived: God is not mocked, for whatever one sows, that will he also reap. For the one who sows to his own flesh will from the flesh reap corruption, but the one who sows to the Spirit will from the Spirit reap eternal life" (Galatians 6:7–8).

We may be able to "play" others and get away with it, but we can never pull one over on our Creator. If you think you can—if you've gotten cocky because you think you're getting away with it—beware! Even if you fool your wife, your parents, your pastor . . . *God* knows what you're doing. And he will not be mocked.

For Reflection:

1. Describe your experiences with guilt. How does it break into your life, sending a dark cloud over the places that should be sunny?

2. What other sinful behaviors are clustered with your sexual sin? Be specific.

3. How do you tend to respond to others when you feel guilty? Do you become angry, impatient, or withdrawn? Who tends to be on the receiving end of these behaviors, and how do you see them affected by your behaviors?

DAY 3: THE REALITY OF SHAME

Along with the sense of guilt, long-term sinful habits or hidden desires create a deep sense of shame. Shame is what happens when we begin to identify directly with our sin and view it as what we *are*, rather than something we *do*. In the face of mounting guilt and an inability to change, our sinful behavior or desires become a source of personal identity. One brother recounted the shame of being called a "jerk off" as a teen because masturbation had been a central part of his life since early childhood. Since he was secretly enslaved to this behavior, living with profound guilt over it for years, in a very deep sense he believed he *was* a "jerk off."

The power of shame is in the hiddenness of our behavior or desires. When we keep things hidden in the dark, shame grows and overwhelms us. We were created by God for intimacy—to be known by others—but in our shame, we're too scared to let others see who we really are, to know the worst things about us. As a result, we live with the nagging sense that if others truly knew us, they would reject us. We become committed to hiding behind a mask and living a lie. We begin to project an illusion for others to see, but this only intensifies the problem. As our hypocrisy increases, so does our shame. As shame deepens, we become more committed to the façade. We enter a relational cycle as destructive and ensnaring as our struggle with sexual sin.

Why is shame so destructive? Because it always results in estrangement from others. Now, this doesn't necessarily mean you are a social outcast. Many people wrestling with deep shame are the "life of the party." Everybody knows and loves them, but inwardly they're hiding, desperately afraid of others discovering their secret. They live with the constant fear of exposure. Although they're well liked, shame makes them think, "Would they really like me if they knew . . . ?" Inwardly they're deeply alone because no one truly knows them. The pressure of living a lie is a crushing burden that often leads to depression, seemingly unrelated anxieties, and other destructive behaviors such as self-harm or substance abuse.

For others, their sense of shame leads to both inward and outward isolation. Instead of living a public life that is a sham, they increasingly withdraw from human community both because of their fear of being found out, and the increasing pain of living with others without being truly known by them.

There is a cost to our souls when we live an illusion before others, never being known for who we truly are.

The only way to find freedom from this cycle is to risk exposure. Listen to the promise of 1 John 1:7: "But if we walk in the light, as he is in the light, we have fellowship with one another, and the blood of Jesus his Son cleanses us from all sin." Did you hear the double promise? If we humble ourselves and risk exposure by walking in the light, instead of hiding in the dark in our shame, God promises we will have fellowship—genuine intimacy—with each other. We'll also get what we've been longing for: cleansing from our sin. The only way out of the cycle of sinful behavior and relational estrangement is to allow ourselves to be truly known. Only honesty and vulnerability with others in the body of Christ delivers us from both shame and slavery to sin.

For Reflection:

1. How does shame manifest itself in your life? Are you outgoing-but-hiding, withdrawn, or something in between?

2. In which relationships are you most hidden? Why? What forms does your hiding take?

3. What do you think would happen if people truly knew you? What are you afraid to lose?

4. On the other hand, what would it be like to be free of hiding—to no longer fear exposure? In what ways would it be a blessing to be "known"?

DAY 4: SEXUAL SIN EMASCULATES US!

Our culture teaches that our masculinity is directly connected to our sexual activity. It celebrates sexual conquest, mocking monogamy in marriage and chastity in singleness. We are told that real men have sex multiple times a week, have had many sexual partners, use porn personally and to spice up their sex lives, etc. The culture is trying to tell us that these chains are a sign of strength. Nothing could be further from the truth.

Sexual sin does not make us more of a man—it emasculates us! We'll discuss this further next week, but know that your sexual sin makes you complicit in injustice, oppressing those who are weaker—those we are called, as men, to cover and protect. It profoundly impacts our view of others.

> **Emasculate [i-mas-kyuh-leyt]**
> verb (used with object)
>   1. to castrate; to remove the testicles of a male animal
>   2. to deprive of strength or vigor, weaken adjective
>   3. deprived of or lacking strength or vigor; effeminate

As a single man, lust affects your ability to engage with others in rich, intentional relationships. Rather than considering how to serve others and lay down your life, lust programs you to view others as commodities, objects that exist for your pleasure. Even if your sin is limited to fantasy and masturbation, you are training yourself in broken, selfish sexuality. Your experience of self-centered sex shapes your expectation for the marriage bed, radically undermining God's design for spouses to serve each other sexually, focusing on the other's pleasure rather than their own. Should God provide a spouse, you will expect sex to be primarily about your pleasure.

For married men, lust robs you of the ability to love your wife and children. You brought selfish expectations of sex into marriage and have taken matters into your own hands when it failed to satisfy. Because sexual sin is such a source of "life" for you, those you are called to love and cherish, shepherd and protect, become an annoyance. They are reduced to obstacles, keeping you from the pleasures you crave.

In the end, sexual sin sucks life and vitality from us. This is part of what is in view when 1 Corinthians 6 describes sexual sin as against our own body. Perhaps more than any other form of sin, it leaves us utterly drained spiritually.

Far from demonstrating our power, sexual sin is a profound revelation of our weakness as we are enslaved to our behaviors and desires. As my colleague Dan says, "A real man can stare down his erection." In other words, he is not a slave to his desires. A real man, empowered by the Spirit, is stronger than his lust.

Further, and in a tragically ironic sense, our pursuit of sexual sin ultimately robs us of our ability to truly enjoy sex, to experience sexual satisfaction. Ephesians 4:18–19 touches on this reality: "They are darkened in their understanding, alienated from the life of God because of the ignorance that is in them, due to their hardness of heart. They have become callous and have given themselves up to sensuality, greedy to practice every kind of impurity." (The fact that Paul is describing pagans in this verse is very significant, and will be discussed during Week 2.)

The Greek word translated as "greedy"—*pleonexia*—literally means a "desire to have more." It is referring to utter insatiability. The NIV translates this as "having a continual lust for more." When we abandon ourselves to indulging in our sexual pleasure, disregarding God's calling and the vows we've made to spouses, the result is slavery. Like a donkey chasing a carrot on a stick, the harder we strive to experience sexual satisfaction, the more it eludes us—even as our reckless pursuit of sexual contentment takes us into deeper and darker perversions. This is what is in view with "every kind of impurity." It means that we will meet with the law of diminishing returns. What once satisfied us no longer does, and we need to go further into the mess to experience the same thrill.

All of us know the brutal experience of sexual sin's bait and switch. You look forward to acting out, carefully putting together the plan. In the moment the act seems glorious, everything you were hoping for. But then . . . it's over. Instantly, the fantasy evaporates and you are left alone with the mess. There could not be a more stark difference between the man you are in your fantasy and the one reaching for the tissue box. But only one of them truly lives in reality . . .

For Reflection:

1. What cultural messages have impacted your understanding of masculinity and sexuality? Do you believe your manhood is determined by your sexual activity? Why or why not?

2. Do you believe that sexual sin is emasculating? How does the man you are in your fantasy life compare to the reality of your experience of slavery? Be specific.

3. Describe your own Ephesians 4:19 encounter with the "insatiableness" of certain desires or behaviors. How have you experienced this downward spiral?

DAY 5: JESUS RESTORES OUR MANHOOD

We'll discuss this in greater detail later on, but realize right now: Jesus' mission is to make us real men! He wants us to be free from enslaving desires and behaviors. He doesn't want us to be emasculated men, but "strengthened with all power, according to his glorious might, for all endurance and patience with joy" (Colossians 1:11).

Jesus invites us to joy and contentment as we learn that the Christian life is best characterized, not by what we *don't* get to do, but by the abundant life Christ offers us. God wants to give us more, not less. Our flesh, the world, and the enemy would have us believe that God is holding out on us, but these are vicious lies against the God who, in love, both created and redeemed us. Jesus describes this contrast poignantly in John 10:10, "The thief comes only to steal and kill and destroy. I came that they may have life and have it abundantly." Brothers, God is not holding out on us in calling us out of our sinful behavior and desires—he wants to give us *life!* He offers to liberate us from our bondage and bring us to sexual sanity.

The irony is, Jesus promises to give us what we're hoping to find in sexual sin. Sex has become an idol for us, but the reality is that our idols are counterfeits that make huge promises, but always fail to deliver. They promise life, but bring only destruction and loss of what is most valuable. They promise excitement and contentment, but eventually lead to emptiness and despair. In a tragic demonstration of the truth of John 10, sexual sin robs us even of the ability to experience sexual fulfilment. As we examined yesterday, we are left only with a "continual lust for more." Pursuit of sexual sin leaves us sexually insatiable and unsatisfied, filled with yearning and discontent.

But here's the rub: Often the Christian life doesn't fit our expectations. It doesn't *seem* like an abundant life. We experience everything from minor disappointments to horrific trauma—even as Christians—that seem to belie the promises offered by Jesus. There are reasons we turn to sexual sin. The challenges of life in a fallen world cause us to question God's goodness and faithfulness. We're tempted to live like orphans, taking matters into our own hands and looking for contentment and comfort wherever we can find it.

But Jesus was straight with us. He *told* us that the Christian life would involve taking up our crosses, denying ourselves, and laying down our lives for his sake and glory. Although some make the declaration, "God loves you and has a wonderful plan for your life," this really needs to be qualified. When Jesus invites you to follow him, he hands you a heavy cross—with splinters—that you're expected to throw up on your shoulder, carry up a steep hill, and when you get to the top . . . they're going to kill you.

But, Jesus' promise to us is that there's a resurrection on the other side of that death. We are called to deny ourselves because the reward he offers is greater than our desires. He says that if you try to save your life you'll lose it, but if you lose it for his sake, you'll find it.

You know the experience of slavery. Sexual sin has robbed you of life and strength—your manhood. Jesus is calling you to a hard road, but a much better road than the one you've chosen to travel—and with a far greater destination. The road of sexual sin leads to all kinds of death, but the road Jesus calls you to walk leads to life now and life forever. As you follow him on this road, you'll begin to experience greater life, joy, strength, and even sexual contentment. Only Jesus can give you what your heart is ultimately longing for!

We began this week by looking at Paul's utter frustration with his sin in Romans 7. But for Paul, it didn't end there. He doesn't stop in a place of despair, but cries out, "Wretched man that I am! Who will deliver me from this body of death? Thanks be to God through Jesus Christ our Lord!" (Romans 7:24–25).

Paul remembers the hope of the gospel, even in the midst of being confounded by his sin. And he goes on from that place of struggle to write one of the most glorious passages in all of Scripture, Romans 8, which radically focuses on what God accomplished for us in Christ and the incredible promises held out to us in the gospel. This is perhaps the most beautiful picture of repentance in the Bible. In the face of his sin and utter inability, Paul begins to *worship*. He reminds himself not only of the forgiveness we have in Christ, but the amazing fullness of our redemption. He begins by declaring "There is therefore now no condemnation" (verse 1) and finishes by proclaiming that nothing can "separate us from the love of God in Christ Jesus our Lord" (verse 39). Throughout this chapter, Paul rehearses the mercy showed to us, the outpouring of the Spirit who intercedes for us because we don't even know how to pray for ourselves, the promise that God will complete his work bringing us to glory, and on and on. In the face of his sin, Paul reminds us of the fullness of life offered to us. He lays hold again of Jesus, gets on his feet and back into the battle against sin.

Jesus wants you to experience freedom and joy. He promises you abundant life and—in the midst of the battle against sin—wants you to discover in him what will truly satisfy your soul. He wants to free you from slavery and show you what it *truly* means to be a man!

For Reflection:

1. How do you define abundant life? In other words, what would make your life really worth living? How might this view lead you to believe that God's "holding out" on you?

2. Do you doubt that Jesus wants you to experience abundant life? Why, and how? In what ways has your experience betrayed the idea of abundant life?

3. What would it mean for you to carry a cross sexually? What would you need to sacrifice? Do you believe that Jesus truly offers you life on the other side of that death? Why or why not?

WEEK 2:
THE PATH INTO THE WASTELAND

KEY CONCEPT: Life is hard! We all know the world is a radically broken place. Because of the fall, suffering—physically, emotionally, and relationally—is the hallmark of our existence. But we're not just passive victims. Through our sexual sin, we perpetuate the curse, poisoning our relationships and exacerbating the brokenness around us.

Regardless of the specifics of our behavior, there is always a context for our sexual sin—loneliness, work pressure, relational strife, financial strain, fear of the future, etc. In the face of life's brokenness, we reject God, and instead embrace sex as our source of comfort and security. But Jesus came to bring restoration to this broken world and redeem our manhood, transforming us from men who oppress and exploit to agents of redemption, bringing healing and extending his kingdom.

DAY 1: LIFE IN A FALLEN WORLD

In the 1991 film *Grand Canyon*, there's a poignant scene where a wealthy man's Lexus breaks down in the middle of a notorious Los Angeles ghetto. Thugs begin to circle as the man waits in a panic for the tow truck to arrive. When the driver, Simon, arrives, he is accosted by one of the gangsters and his nine-millimeter pistol. Simon humbly asks to be able to do his job and tow the car away. As they talk, Simon makes a profound comment on life as we know it, "Man, the world ain't supposed to work like this . . . I'm supposed to be able to do my job without asking you if I can. That dude is supposed to be able to wait with his car without you rippin' him off. Everything's supposed to be different than what it is." Indeed, we live in a world that has been profoundly impacted by the fall. Every aspect of life has been affected. Nothing is unstained. It's *not* supposed to be this way.

Living in a fallen world means suffering. There is no way around that reality. Although there are extreme cases—disabilities, abuse, oppression, discrimination—everyone has endured suffering on some level. Therefore, every person could build a case for why they have the right to grumble about their circumstances—forever.

But here's the thing: We're part of that fallen world. Our negative response to suffering adds to the brokenness of the world we live in. We can't get around the fact that we are a part of the problem. As Paul David Tripp is fond of saying, "We trouble our trouble." We find ourselves in broken situations, but our sinful responses perpetuate the curse.

For many of us, sexual sin becomes a way to find escape from the pressures of life, or to add excitement to our humdrum existence. Some of us are tempted to act out when faced with an important deadline, or as a way of getting back at our spouse after a fight. Others use sexual sin to celebrate an accomplishment. Singles often use fantasy and masturbation to relieve the pain of loneliness, while married men often want to escape from the challenges faced in relationship with a real person. The people we objectify in our fantasies never cross us or thwart our desires. They exist for one purpose—to satisfy us. There is always *some* context for our sin.

There are innumerable reasons why we pursue sexual sin at any given time, but in some way we are trying to find "life" in sin. I've heard men say that they felt like kids on Christmas morning as they looked forward to their next opportunities to act out. They're excited over their sin like nothing else in life.

This is often how we live, even as Christians. We sing hymns and worship songs that exalt God, declaring with the psalmist that his "steadfast love is better than life" (Psalm 63:3). This is our official theology. But the way we live demonstrates another allegiance. Our sexual sin reveals our functional theology. Here's another way to think about it: Your true religion is what you delight in. The things that most excite your heart and make life worth living are pointers toward where you place your ultimate hope.

For Reflection:

1. In what ways have you experienced the brokenness of this world? Give a brief description.

2. What current circumstances cause you stress, anxiety, or pressure? What is the connection between the challenges you face and your sexual struggles?

3. What's your response to the statement: "Your religion is what you delight in"? In what ways does your sexual behavior reflect what you find worth living for?

DAY 2: REJECTION OF THE LIVING WATER

Because of the pain of life in a fallen world, some Christians believe that sin is not unavoidable, but futile to *try* to avoid. It is seen as an understandable response to our unmet needs. But the Bible describes the situation very differently: Sin is the refusal to submit to God's will for me, the throwing off of his fetters to establish my own rule over my own life. Jeremiah 2:9–13 describes it this way,

> Therefore I still contend with you,
> declares the LORD,
>   and with your children's children I will contend.
> For cross to the coasts of Cyprus and see,
>   or send to Kedar and examine with care;
>   see if there has been such a thing.
> Has a nation changed its gods,
>   even though they are no gods?
> But my people have changed their glory
>   for that which does not profit.
> Be appalled, O heavens, at this;
>   be shocked, be utterly desolate,
> declares the LORD,
> for my people have committed two evils:
> they have forsaken me,
>   the fountain of living waters,
> and hewed out cisterns for themselves,
>   broken cisterns that can hold no water.

Jeremiah records God's incredulous response to his people's rebellion. He calls them to search far and wide to find another nation that has ever abandoned its gods. Even though the idols of the nations are worthless frauds, their worshippers are actually more faithful than Israel, who should be worshipping the one true God. Therefore, God's people are condemned on two counts: 1) they turned from "the fountain of living waters"—the God who created and sustains them and invites them to find life in him; and 2) they tried to make life work on their terms and take care of themselves, even though the attempt was utterly futile.

Although we no longer bow down to statues or build little shrines, we continue to seek life from the created world. We look to relationships, work, toys, sports, and entertainment to satisfy our souls. Of course, sex has been one of the most significant ways we've turned from God and his calling in order to live as we want—often with disastrous results. We abandon the icy, refreshing stream flowing down from the mountain of God, choosing instead the lukewarm, rank water we store for ourselves in our desert cisterns.

Why do we do this? We want control. Life on our terms. We are created to be dependent on God, but we want independence. When you make a cistern and fill it, you know where you stand, exactly how much water you have. With a fresh spring, you have to trust it will continue flowing, that it will be there when you need it. For a variety of reasons, we don't like to live by faith. Rather than praying for daily bread, we are accustomed to a stocked refrigerator.

For many, the whole focus of life is to work like crazy and max out their 401k, so they have the security to live out their final decades on earth in prosperous ease. As we saw yesterday, over the years we've learned that God usually doesn't follow our game plan. Because suffering is a reality, we've discovered God's plan is often painful. Being a Christian doesn't mean we've found the easy ticket in this life. It means carrying a cross and taking the nails.

There is a tragic irony here: We don't want to be dependent on the fountain of living water, but our attempts at independence don't work. The water we're so desperate to store is actually worse for us and—since the cisterns leak—rapidly disappears. We spent a lot of time last week considering the destructive folly of sexual sin. It makes great promises, but doesn't deliver. It offers life, but destroys what is most valuable in this world. We long for strength and affirmation, but sexual sin emasculates us. And all the while fresh, living water continues to pour down from the heights.

You need to see this: Sexual sin is idolatry! It is a rejection of God, attempting to make life work on your terms. It is not somehow worse than other sins, but it is something God takes very seriously, because our involvement in sexual sin is fundamentally rebellion against him. In the Old Testament, God likened Israel's idolatry to adultery. Sexual sin is idolatry, and continues to be spiritual adultery against God. Consider Paul's words from 1 Thessalonians 4:3–8:

For this is the will of God, your sanctification: that you abstain from
sexual immorality; that each one of you know how to control his
own body in holiness and honor, not in the passion of lust like the
Gentiles who do not know God; that no one transgress and wrong
his brother in this matter, because the Lord is an avenger in all these
things, as we told you beforehand and solemnly warned you. For God
has not called us for impurity, but in holiness. Therefore whoever
disregards this, disregards not man but God, who gives his Holy
Spirit to you.

This passage clearly spells it out: Unrestrained sexual behavior is what
pagans do! What you do with your penis matters—it is a demonstration of
your spiritual allegiance. Pagans are those who reject God and give themselves
over to their sexual appetites. They have no restraint over their bodies. They
are controlled by their desires. Are you characterized as one who "control[s]
his own body in holiness and honor," or are you ruled by the "passion of lust"
like the pagans?

Even as Christians, we can be controlled by lust. In the passage quoted
earlier, Jeremiah was writing to God's people on the eve of their exile. They
had rebelled against God and were about to fall under his judgment. The
Babylonians descended and conquered Jerusalem. The Israelites were taken
into captivity. They were removed from the Promised Land and sent into exile.
In the same way, our sexual sin undermines our allegiance to Christ. We fail
to live in the fullness of life offered to us by Jesus because we have chosen a
false god to worship. Like the Israelites, we choose leaky cisterns over living
water—and the results are devastating.

It is important to note that this passage was written to *Christians*! You are
not alone in your struggle with sexual sin. God's people have always needed
to experience redemption in this area of life. These words were written to the
church in Thessalonica because they needed to hear them—and so do we. You
are not under condemnation because of your struggle with sexual sin, but you
need to see the starkness of the situation. It is idolatry, and Jesus calls you to
radical devotion to him.

For Reflection:

1. Do you agree that sexual sin is idolatry? When do you turn to sexual sin instead of to God, and in what ways?

2. How does it make you feel to realize that your behavior characterizes that of pagans?

3. Can you identify other places in your life, besides sex, that function as "leaky cisterns" for you? Consider things you delight in. Do these activities lead you to worship the Giver of good gifts, or become objects of worship? Give examples.

DAY 3: LEAKY CISTERNS AND BROKEN MASCULINITY

Again, sexual sin is idolatry. It is a violation of the first Great Commandment to love God, as well as a violation of the second Great Commandment to love others as ourselves (Matthew 22:34–40; Mark 12:28–34). Sexual sin is *always* exploitive. It always takes those made in the image of God and turns them into objects for my pleasure. Do you see how the violations of these commands hang together? We exploit others (violating the second command) and, in the same moment, long to be personally exalted (violating the first command).

At first glance, it may appear that the individual on the monitor, the dancer, etc., is the focus of our idolatry. But think about it: What goes on in your fantasies? You're creating a world where everyone exists to serve, adore, and please *you*! That is the great offense of sexual sin. In a very tangible way, we set ourselves up as little gods and pretend others are ours to rule. In our minds we refashion the universe, throwing God out of the picture, placing ourselves at the center, and populating it with God's creatures to worship us.

This is yet another way that sexual sin radically undercuts our masculinity. As men, we are called to cover and protect others, especially women and children. We are created to be guardians over the weak. It is a blasphemous twisting of God's design that we cease to be protectors, instead using our strength to oppress others, turning them into objects to consume sexually. In Ezekiel 34, God brings a stinging indictment against the leaders of Israel, describing them as shepherds who devour their sheep, rather than feeding them. When we engage in sexual sin, we are guilty of the same charge. We exploit those we are called to care for.

Depending on what behaviors you engage in, this oppression can be either blatant or subtle. Perhaps this seems a little abstract. How exactly are *you* charged to care for the model on the page, or the actor in the video? As we'll examine in more depth later, men were created to serve and care for others. When you partake in pornography, you are participating in the oppression. Just because you are not behind the camera, you're not absolved of guilt. Most people in the porn industry (men and women) suffered sexual abuse, some as young children. There is a history of pain and exploitation behind the seductive eyes and pretense of pleasure.

Of course, when your behavior involves physical contact with others, the offense is more obvious. Whether prostitution or a long-term affair, in our sin we take advantage of those who are weaker—even when they're willing and enthusiastic participants—for our own selfish ends. This oppression is in stark contrast to who God calls you to be as a man!

Although this often sounds sexist in today's culture, men's greater physical strength is part of God's design, so that we might cover and protect those who are weaker, particularly in the context of marriage (1 Peter 3:6). Similarly, he is called to be the spiritual head of his wife (Ephesians 5:22–33). This doesn't mean that men are better, or more spiritually mature, than women. To be head ultimately means to reflect Jesus by laying down our lives for our spouses. In fact, our tendency toward passivity since the fall probably contributes to God's command that we lead. He knows that in our sin, most of us are naturally bent to sit back and let women take charge. Although bad teaching on gender roles has caused great harm, when a man follows God's calling, dying to self to serve like Jesus, there is no exploitation. Women are blessed and able to flourish, not treated as servants. In Christ, there is no male and female. There is a fundamental equality among all citizens of the kingdom.

When we live in sexual sin, we are violating who we are created to be. First Corinthians 6:18 says, "Flee from sexual immorality. Every other sin a person commits is outside the body, but the sexually immoral person sins against his own body." There are a lot of implications with that statement. We've already looked at the reality of diminishing returns and our inability to experience sexual satisfaction. But sexual sin also makes us operate radically contrary to God's design for us as men. Sexual sin not only emasculates us through robbing us of strength and enslaving our souls, it places us outside God's design and calling, becoming lesser men, less truly human as his image-bearers—and more like brute beasts. We rob ourselves not only of the good gift and righteous pleasure that God extends through sexuality, but we diminish ourselves as those created to uniquely "image" him in this fallen world.

All this matters deeply to God. Those we exploit are his creation. They exist to honor and serve him, not us. Remember the scary declaration from yesterday, "the Lord is an avenger in all these things" (1 Thessalonians 4:6). Jesus is returning to settle the score with his enemies. Read through the glorious description of Jesus' triumphant return in Revelation 19:11–21, then ask yourself: Whose side would you want to be on?

And this is crucial: The verses immediately before describe Jesus' wedding feast. Those we exploit are not mere creatures—the equivalent of God's pets. They are his bride! If the life of an adulterer is in danger from an enraged, betrayed husband, how much greater are our souls in peril if we take lightly our violation of Jesus' betrothed?

What does this mean for those of us who are in Christ and continue to oppress others sexually? Hear again this warning: "Do not be deceived: God is not mocked, for whatever one sows, that will he also reap. For the one who sows to his own flesh will from the flesh reap corruption, but the one who sows to the Spirit will from the Spirit reap eternal life" (Galatians 6:7–8). Remember, your sexuality is a litmus test for your spirituality.

In the first century the Jewish leaders blew off Jesus' warning because they were the physical offspring of Abraham. But the New Testament makes clear that the true Israelite is spiritually, not physically, generated. In the same way, I fear many in the 21st century American church have a very flip view of their sin because they're "under grace." The Bible always assumes that those in Christ will increasingly live as members of his kingdom, the new created order. Our lives will bear fruit that comes from the heart, not mere outward deeds. If you continue to sin sexually, brother, I urge you to take it extremely seriously. Jesus hates what you are doing and is an avenger of the oppressed. It may be that your sexual behavior demonstrates what is ultimately most true of your spiritual state—much more than your formal profession of faith!

But be encouraged: You wouldn't be reading these words if you weren't seeking change on some level. The Christian life is a tightrope. Our hope is never our performance, but only the grace and mercy of God. At the same time, his power is at work to effect change, and we should expect our lives to grow and bear fruit.

For Reflection:

1. How has your sexual sin eroded your calling as a man? In what specific ways are you "devouring" others rather than "feeding" them? Which relationships have been most affected by your behavior?

2. How would your relationships change if you fulfilled your calling and design as a man to selflessly serve and protect others? Give examples.

3. What's your reaction to the fact that God is an avenger of the exploited? What does your sexuality say about your spirituality?

DAY 4: THE EROSION OF INTIMACY

Sexual sin radically impacts our interactions with others. First, because of shame, we tend to avoid deep, intimate relationships. Our shame keeps us on the run, scared to let anyone get too close. At the same time, we long for connection with others, so in our sexual insanity we try to connect in a way that doesn't "cost" us anything. We want to experience the benefits of relationship without having to be personally vulnerable.[3]

Because we fear genuine intimacy, fallout will occur in our relationships, and in very concrete ways. Those closest to you will be most severely damaged. Your marriage will not be the deep, one-flesh intimacy God designed. There are also huge ramifications for your sex life. Inasmuch as your focus is on the physical aspect of sex, apart from God's deeper design, you will grow increasingly dissatisfied—especially as the years go by and your wife can't stack up against the eternal youth of pornography.

Similarly, if you struggle with same-sex attraction, the physical focus will keep you perpetually discontent. You won't rejoice in the spouse God has given you; instead, you'll be forever conscious of what he's withholding from you. Focusing exclusively on the physical pleasure of sex falls woefully short of God's design for sexuality to reflect and celebrate the deeper emotional and spiritual intimacy between a husband and wife—not to mention the echoing whispers of the divine imbued into sexuality by its creator.

As we examined yesterday, sexual sin trains us to see others as commodities. For single men, this is particularly poignant because it conditions what you seek in a spouse. Your sights will be out of focus as you give significant consideration to who you believe will bring sexual satisfaction (a focus on the physical), while devaluing a woman's spiritual and emotional maturity. Also, as discussed last week, your response to guilt and shame will color your interactions with others, perhaps even undermining your ability to pursue a spouse. Living in the real world with other people is radically different than the fantasies we concoct. Over time, most prefer to live increasingly in the unreality of their inner (or online) fantasy life.

Sexual sin forces us to become emotionally distant. For singles, this means avoiding any depth of relationship—not only with the opposite sex, but also with male peers. Many men are already uncomfortable with deeper emotional intimacy, and sexual sin–with its layers of guilt and shame—further exacerbates the problem. We avoid people who probe too deeply. We refuse to let others truly know us, and instead hide behind the smokescreen of work, ministry, or service. The deeper and darker our hidden sin, the more fearful we are of exposure. This leads to either isolation or a more elaborate façade. It's hard to say which is more destructive to your soul, but both responses are two sides of the same coin—keeping others at arm's length, refusing to enter deeply into relationship.

Marriage is most devastated by sexual sin as it radically undermines God's design for deep oneness. Because we are committed to deceitfully covering our tracks, we're forced to withdraw from our spouses. Here's what happens: as soon as we have something to hide, we zealously guard that area of life. As sexual sin grows, consuming more time, energy, and money, there is more to "protect" from your wife. As this pattern continues, we reach a point where no topic of conversation is safe. There are just too many trails we need to keep hidden so we won't be exposed .

The result? Interaction with our spouse is limited to the kids, work, and home improvement projects. We focus on topics that are emotionally detached from us as individuals, and particularly on our relationship as husband and wife. Eventually the connection is no deeper than the superficial banter around the office water cooler. Even the most important issues are discussed from a place of emotional detachment. We don't want to be exposed and are often too selfish to care about the emotions of our spouse. We become unwilling to engage her heart and pursue her emotionally because we're terrified that she'll get behind our wall and really know us.

This emotional estrangement grows over the years, until your spouse feels like she's living with a total stranger. Often she's unable to put her finger on the problem; she just knows that there's no sense of real closeness. Combine this emotional estrangement with a husband's denials and insinuations that the problems are in her head and you're left with a very hurting wife, questioning her sanity and her marriage.

There is huge fallout for your children as well. As sexual sin saps your vitality, you will not be the loving, engaged father you want to be. You'll likely find yourself getting increasingly irritated and impatient with your kids. As your annoyance grows, they'll begin to withdraw. The small child who cheerfully met you at the door crying "Daddy! Daddy!" becomes the sullen, withdrawn teenager who doesn't even want to be in the same room with you. Although you might diligently plan for their future and set up a college savings account, it's unlikely you'll pursue their hearts. Helping kids process the quagmire of their adolescent years is taxing on any parent, but all the more when your spiritual vitality is depleted by sexual sin. Teaching them about the Christian faith won't be a top priority when you feel like a hypocrite and a failure—perhaps even questioning the validity of the faith. As with your wife, you won't pursue your children on a deep, emotional level. They too will feel like they're living with a stranger.

For Reflection:

1. In what ways has deceit impacted your closest relationships? Describe specific instances where your hiding has inhibited real conversation with others.

2. What does your façade look like? How does it differ from who you are in secret?

3. What do you believe would be the cost of rebuilding intimacy, allowing those closest to you to know your deepest struggles—letting go of the sin you love, losing your image, facing the possibility of significant fallout in your relationships?

DAY 5: REBIRTH IN THE WASTELAND

This week began by describing the world as a radically broken place. We are born into a fallen world where things "ain't supposed to work like this." It's true that the problem didn't begin with us. The Bible describes us as born into sin's slavery. As sons of Adam, all of us are plagued with original sin. We are born stuck in sin. It's natural to us. In each of us is a fierce independence that rejects the authority of God, and a brute selfishness that looks out for number one rather than caring for others. As little children, before we are even clearly conscious of right and wrong, the trajectory was set for us to live for self, turning our backs on God and exploiting our fellow man. And as we saw when we looked at Romans 7 last week, even in Christ we continue to battle against our flesh.

But we are not innocent victims of Adam's sin. Although original sin is a reality, over time we become guilty accomplices to the brokenness. Once exploited by others, we become exploiters. A dear friend who suffered horrific sexual abuse as a child saw this dynamic in her own heart and wrote, "Bitten, I did bite; and agreed with Death to pass the poison on."

Despite the reality of original sin and the ways we suffer in life because of the sins of others, Scripture teaches that we are responsible for our actions. Romans 1:18–20 teaches that all men are without excuse because God's presence and power are evident in the world he made. All of creation calls us to see, "I AM!" but we harden our hearts against his presence so that we might live pursuing the selfish desires of our heart.

Jesus' work of redemption includes becoming the leader of a new people. In his resurrection, Jesus became the fulfillment of God's intended design for humanity. Jesus doesn't restore us to Adam's pre-fallen state—he goes infinitely beyond that to become who Adam would have become if he'd never sinned and had instead received the invitation at last to eat from the Tree of Life.

Here's our reality: Apart from Christ's radical intervention we had absolutely no hope. There was no choice but to continue in sin. As Christians, God's rescue mission in our lives has begun. It is not completed at our salvation, although the eventual result is guaranteed. At salvation, God begins the work he promises to bring to completion (see Philippians 1:6). We can be confident he will complete this work; Scripture is filled with promises to that effect. One of my favorites is Hebrews 10:14: "For by a single offering he has perfected for all time those who are being sanctified."

Growing as a Christian is a lifelong process of becoming who God intends us to be, for all eternity. A significant aspect of this glory is that he transforms us into men who no longer exploit others and pass on the curse, but like Jesus begin to lay down our lives for others and become his ambassadors of reconciliation. Through us, God makes his appeal to this broken world and moves his kingdom forward (see 2 Corinthians 5:17–20). Brother, he is inviting you to a radically transformed and glorious existence!

Another irony of sexual sin is that we settle for so much less than the blessing God has for us, all the while becoming more miserable and enslaved in the process. I love this well-worn quote by C. S. Lewis, and will close this week out with it. Take some time to meditate upon it:

> "We are half-hearted creatures, fooling about with drink and sex
> and ambition when infinite joy is offered us, like an ignorant child
> who wants to go on making mud pies in a slum because he cannot
> imagine what is meant by the offer of a holiday at the sea."[4]

For Reflection:

1. In what ways have you passed the poison on to others? Be specific.

2. Do you believe that God is truly offering you "a holiday at the sea"? Do you believe he is a God of pleasure? What experience causes you to doubt this?

3. What do you think it would be like to pass on the blessing of Christ's kingdom instead of the curse? What concrete changes would happen in your relationships, behavior, work habits?

WEEK 3:
THORNBUSHES IN THE WASTELAND

KEY CONCEPT: A map is a great tool—if you know how to use it. First, in order to interpret a map correctly, you must know the points of the compass. Equally important, you need to know where you are on the map, which direction you're facing and where you're planning to go.

The intent of the past two weeks was to give you a sense of where you are and the miserable condition of the place, so you'll be motivated to move. This week, as well as in all of Section 2, we'll focus on understanding the points of the compass—looking at the work of Christ and considering the difference that his death and resurrection make for those struggling with sexual sin. This week introduces a biblical model of "why we do what we do" and the hope for lasting change, using the metaphor of a tree. The goal is to help you map your life so you can begin moving forward.

DAY 1: THE FRUIT

The Bible describes our lives as sowing seed—declaring that all our decisions, actions, and words will reap some kind of harvest (see especially Galatians 6:7–9). In keeping with this theme, the Bible often uses agricultural metaphors to describe humanity, both positively and negatively: Let's review just a couple of them.

> Blessed is the man
> who walks not in the counsel of the wicked,
> nor stands in the way of sinners,
> nor sits in the seat of scoffers;
> but his delight is in the law of the LORD,
> and on his law he meditates day and night.
> He is like a tree
> planted by streams of water

that yields its fruit in its season,
  and its leaf does not wither.
In all that he does, he prospers.
The wicked are not so,
  but are like chaff that the wind drives away.
Therefore the wicked will not stand in the judgment,
  nor sinners in the congregation of the righteous;
for the LORD knows the way of the righteous,
  but the way of the wicked will perish (Psalm 1).

Thus says the LORD:
"Cursed is the man who trusts in man
  and makes flesh his strength,
  whose heart turns away from the LORD.
He is like a shrub in the desert,
  and shall not see any good come.
He shall dwell in the parched places of the wilderness,
  in an uninhabited salt land.
"Blessed is the man who trusts in the LORD,
  whose trust is the LORD.
He is like a tree planted by water,
  that sends out its roots by the stream,
and does not fear when heat comes,
  for its leaves remain green,
and is not anxious in the year of drought,
  for it does not cease to bear fruit."
The heart is deceitful above all things,
  and desperately sick;
  who can understand it?
"I the LORD search the heart
  and test the mind,
to give every man according to his ways,
according to the fruit of his deeds." (Jeremiah 17:5–10)

What do these passages tell us? They describe our behavior as fruit. Some trees blossom and bear fruit regardless of their circumstances. Those with deep roots in God and his promises flourish no matter what chaos swirls around them. But Psalm 1 says those who resist him, living for self and disregarding his call on their lives, are like chaff—the part of the grain that is worthless, even weightless. It is simply blown away, carried off by the breeze as the stalks of wheat are beaten to yield their grain.

Similarly, Jeremiah describes those who turn to false comforts in the face of life's pressures, declaring they will not bear fruit. Instead, they are like a scrub brush growing in the desert, withered and parched by the heat like a dry, thorny briar patch. In this passage, Israel is desperately looking to surrounding nations like Egypt to help them face the Babylonian invasion, rather than trusting in God to deliver them. History proved Egypt to be an impotent ally, as she too was conquered by Nebuchadnezzar's forces.

As we read last week in Jeremiah 2, there are two ways we sin against God: We outwardly, brazenly reject him through our behavior; and in our rebellion, we try to find some other way to make life work for us. Idolatry is always a blatant rejection of God, as we try to make life work on our terms.

Viewing all of our behavior as fruit, some of it is clearly rotten—for example, all the ways we act out sexually (the reasons you picked up this book in the first place). But it goes much further, encompassing all the relational fallout resulting from sexual sin—lying, angry outbursts, avoiding genuine intimacy with others, squandering our God-given resources. And there is a myriad of seemingly less destructive comforts we love to turn to: sports, entertainment, food, hobbies. At least initially, we turn to sexual sin only after these lesser pleasures have failed to satisfy the craving of our hearts.

We also produce artificial fruit—fruit that appeals to the eye, but is fake. No matter how genuine it may appear, it has zero value beyond a good appearance. Artificial fruit is doing the right thing for the wrong reason— serving in ministry to cover our shame, bringing our wife flowers because we feel guilty for looking at porn at work, making sure we get back on track with our Bible reading after a major sexual fall. These are all good things in themselves, but if we do them apart from living truthfully about our struggle with sin, they're essentially forms of penance. We're creating a mirage. It's wonderful to bring your wife flowers, but she'd rather you were honest about how you've sinned against her. It's glorious to serve in the children's ministry, but church leaders should first and foremost be shepherding you through your struggle with sexual sin. God delights to meet with you, but he wants you to come humbly yet boldly in the righteousness of Christ, not slinking back to him shamefacedly with your tail between your legs.

God created and redeemed us to bear fruit that would bless others and honor him. Jesus described himself as the true vine, saying that we are branches grafted into him, bearing fruit as we abide in him (see John 15:1–8). As you're dealing with the sexual sin and other idols in your life, Jesus is pruning you to bear fruit that brings life to others, extending his kingdom. He wants to restore us to sanity in every aspect of life. It is a glorious calling, which in stark relief exposes the emptiness and futility of our broken sexuality.

For Reflection:

1. Does your life resemble a flourishing tree or a briar patch—or a combination of the two? Explain.

2. Besides sexual sin, what other false comforts do you pursue? Consider activities or hobbies that tend to cause friction with your spouse, family members, or friends.

3. Where are you cultivating artificial fruit? How does this manifest itself? In which relationships are you most prone to do the right things for the wrong reason, and what does that look like specifically?

DAY 2: THE SEED

"As in water face reflects face, so the heart of man reflects the man" (Proverbs 27:19).

If the fruit of our tree is our behavior, the result of all the decisions we make, where does our behavior come from? The Bible teaches that it comes from your heart. Consider these passages:

> For out of the heart come evil thoughts, murder, adultery, sexual immorality, theft, false witness, slander. (Matthew 15:19)

> No good tree bears bad fruit, nor does a bad tree bear good fruit. Each tree is recognized by its own fruit. People do not pick figs from thornbushes, or grapes from briers. The good man brings good things out of the good stored up in his heart, and the evil man brings evil things out of the evil stored up in his heart. For out of the overflow of his heart his mouth speaks. (Luke 6:43–45 NIV)

According to Scripture, our heart is the center of our will, from which all our decisions and actions pour forth. That's why Proverbs 4:23 warns, "Keep your heart with all vigilance, for from it flow the springs of life." Our heart has the potential to gush either pure, clean living water, or raw sewage.

But our hearts aren't neutral. Yesterday, we looked at Jeremiah 17:9: "The heart is deceitful above all things, and desperately sick; who can understand it?" The Bible describes us as conceived in sin and sinful from birth (see Psalm 51:5). Perhaps the starkest indictment against humanity is the statement just prior to the flood in Genesis 6:5, "The LORD saw that the wickedness of man was great in the earth, and that every intention of the thoughts of his heart was only evil continually." This is what theologians refer to as original sin. It's what it means to be a son of Adam. Since his fall, we walk lock-step from infancy in his rebellious ways. It is what comes naturally to us.

And it goes even further. Why do we bear the artificial fruit we talked about yesterday? Because even our good works are naturally tainted. For many, the doctrine of "total depravity" doesn't ring true, because they see many thoughtful, caring people in the world. But total depravity doesn't mean we're a bunch of little Hitlers running around trying to conquer the world and slaughter innocent people. It refers to the reality that the fall has tainted every aspect of who we are. That's why Isaiah describes even our righteous deeds as "a polluted garment" (Isaiah 64:6). Some commentators suggest this could refer to menstrual cloth. Apart from Christ, all our good deeds have at least a little bit of self— assuaging guilt, building up our good reputation, feeding our pride (because *I* serve more than *them*), encouraging self-righteousness. This is why wise preachers in the past called God's people to repent of their "holy works."

So what does it mean to guard our hearts? One of my friends describes it this way: He used to think it meant blocking his heart against any foreign intruder, standing guard before it, with rifle raised. Now, understanding the deceitfulness of his heart, he realizes it means keeping his heart before him at all times, with the sights of his rifle trained on it!

For Reflection:

1. Do you believe in original sin? Why or why not? Whether you believe in it or not, what evidence do you see in your own life that would support the idea?

2. Do you believe in the idea of total depravity? Why or why not? How would this doctrine explain the world, and your own life?

3. In what ways are even your "holy works" tainted? Describe an occasion when you did some "good" thing more for the sake of self than for others.

DAY 3: THE SOIL

This fallen seed does not exist in a vacuum, but is planted in the soil of a fallen world. The soil is everything in your life outside your control. Some things are specific to you as a person. For example, you were born male, with unchangeable physical characteristics and a personality that is largely innate, at least since you were very young. You have certain gifts and abilities, and lack others you wish you had. These things deeply impact us. There are expectations that culture and family place on males—and sometimes we don't fit.

Further, the messages we receive about masculinity often spur us on in our pursuit of sin and folly. (We'll dig more into this in Week 7.) Most of us wrestle with what it means to be a man, and search for ways to assert our masculinity. For example, I was never an athlete but I pursued everything from sexual promiscuity to alcohol and drugs, to driving a truck, to working as a lumberjack—all in a feeble attempt to prove my manhood. (STDs, arrests, accidents and bodily injury ensued.) Many men struggle with the physical bodies God has given them, or feel insecure about their intelligence—because we perceive we have too little *or* too much. Some of us are naturally outgoing, born leaders, while others hate the spotlight and social situations. Some are driven, striving for success in everything; others are content to amble along, taking life as it comes. Regardless of your specific personality and gifts, you possess exactly what God intended and declared very good for you. At the same time, all of these traits are impacted by the fall and need redemption in Christ.

Other soil conditions are similarly outside our control, but not distinct to our person—the family we were born into, our specific cultural group, and the impact of wider American society. Interactions with peers—especially when we're young—and the reality of peer pressure are very formative. Some of us have experienced extreme trauma—physical, emotional, and/or sexual—in our homes, our extended families, or at school.

And within the context of a Christian worldview, we live in a cosmos at war. We are surrounded by unseen spiritual forces, with an enemy bent on our destruction (more on this in Week 7 too). There are two dangers when we consider our spiritual enemy. One is to be too focused on that reality—overly concerned and fearful (when Jesus is infinitely more powerful), or enamored by darkness. The other danger is to disregard this reality and live as if you don't have an enemy constantly battling against your soul, seeking to seduce, condemn, and rob you of joy, rendering you ineffective for the kingdom of Christ.[5]

This is a *huge* category. Each aspect of it requires careful reflection, well beyond this week. Here's the bottom line: you are not merely the sum total of all the individual decisions you make. The aspects of life outside your control are extremely significant and impact you as an individual.

That said, our life history is not determinative. We don't examine these things so we can point fingers and make excuses for our present behavior. Nonetheless, we are often blind to the ways that we live as slaves to the past— persisting in behavioral patterns, ways of thinking, and beliefs that were either directly taught or came about as ways of coping with life in our specific broken situations. We will only grow as men, and be free from the brokenness of our past, if we're willing to face the toxicity of our unique soil and turn to Jesus for redemption. Our default is to ignore these realities or pretend they don't affect us, but that lie keeps us in chains.

For Reflection:

1. Which soil conditions specific to your person have most impacted you— understanding of maleness, physical characteristics, personality and gifts? Which ones do you wish you could change? How have you tried to change them?

2. Briefly describe life in your home growing up. Were both parents present? How did they demonstrate love and affection toward one another—or did they? What was your relationship like with your dad and mom? Did you have siblings, and if so how did you get along with them then, and now?

3. Which of the remaining soil conditions—cultural or societal influences such as specific ethnic group, where you lived, socio-economic factors, peer pressure, or spiritual oppression—most impacted your life? In what ways?

DAY 4: THE ROOTS

The roots represent the desires of our hearts—the ways we try to connect and feed off the soil we're placed in. Although our desires in themselves are not sinful, the problem is that we try to satisfy them from creation alone, apart from God. Our desires were intended to draw us deeper into relationship with God and each other, but they run amuck when we go to created things for life, rather than to the God who *is* the life-giver.

So what are some of the desires God has built within us? First, as God's image-bearers, we were created to rule over this world as his stewards. As a result, we long to make a difference in the world, for our lives to make an impact. Why are so many men frustrated in their careers, feeling like they're in dead-end jobs? Because we want our lives to count for *something*. We were created to rule over this earth, to take dominion and subdue it (Genesis 1:26–28). This aspect of our image-bearing can be a blessing as we work and relate to others in meaningful ways, but it can become corporate greed, political power-grabbing, and in the extreme, even attempts at world domination.

Further, we were created for community. When God created Adam and set him in the garden before the Fall, the first thing he declared "not good" was Adam's aloneness. Until that point, God had been thoroughly pleased with his creative work (see Genesis 2:18f). You know the story: God put Adam to sleep, formed Eve from his rib, woke him up and presented her . . . and he was delighted!

Now, God's displeasure with Adam's aloneness does not mean that his plan is for everyone to marry. To the contrary, Scripture actually urges unmarried people to remain single for the sake for the kingdom. (Check out 1 Corinthians 7:6–8, 32–35, a passage you won't hear taught in most American, suburban churches.) But it does point to the reality that we need community. This is another aspect of our image-bearing. We are created for community because we're made in the image of our Triune God who existed in community from eternity past. God in three persons means he never existed alone. Like him, we are designed to live in relationship with others.

Rightly exercised, our desires bring blessing, but in a fallen world they can be horrifically broken. This is particularly true with our relationships. We're often desperate to have another creature fill the emptiness in our soul that only

God can fill. The euphoric rush of falling in love frequently consists of two people living under the delusion that the other person will make his or her life worth living. Eventually expectations are dashed and we learn to find our joy and contentment in God as we choose to persevere with this flawed individual (especially if we've pursued marriage), or we embark on another crazy crusade for the one who will satisfy our souls.

Finally, similar to our desire for community, we were created to experience intimacy. Far deeper than sexuality, intimacy is truly knowing another and being deeply known in return. We were created to live free from shame, not fearing what others would think if they really knew us. Psalm 139 captures this beautifully:

> O LORD, you have searched me and known me!
> You know when I sit down and when I rise up;
>   you discern my thoughts from afar.
> You search out my path and my lying down
>   and are acquainted with all my ways.
> Even before a word is on my tongue,
>   behold, O LORD, you know it altogether.
> You hem me in, behind and before,
>   and lay your hand upon me.
> Such knowledge is too wonderful for me;
>   it is high; I cannot attain it. (Psalm 139:1–6)

Most of us do not delight that God knows every word before we utter it, that he has shared every thought we've ever had. But it leads David to worship. Why? Because for David—who was no stranger to sexual sin—this profoundly demonstrates God's nearness, the depth of his intimacy with us. God knows every thought—not because he's keeping a tally for judgment day, but because he actually loves you that much! He's paying attention. You are truly that known and delighted in. That's why Paul, anticipating eternity in 1 Corinthians 13:12, declares, "I shall know fully, even as I have been fully known." There's a glory and wonder to God's deep, intimate knowledge of us in Christ.

Have you ever accomplished something—maybe a home-improvement project or a difficult task at work—and wanted to share your accomplishment with others? There is one who observes every moment of your life, who wants to rejoice in all your triumphs, comfort and strengthen you in your trials, and pull you up when you stumble and fall. David's confidence in God's goodness and mercy enables him to end his psalm by saying, "Search me, O God, and know my heart! Try me and know my thoughts! And see if there be any grievous way in me, and lead me in the way everlasting!" (Psalm 139:23–24). Understanding who God truly is and our relationship to him through Christ frees us to fearlessly pray this same prayer, confidently drawing near to the throne of grace so that we may receive mercy and find grace to help in our time of need (see Hebrews 4:16).

These three categories manifest themselves in a variety of subtle ways. We desire to be affirmed. We want to be number one in someone's life. We long for security, comfort, and affection—to be loved and understood. We want a sense of control and a life free from emotional and physical pain and suffering.

There is nothing inherently wrong with these desires. The problem is that they quickly morph into demands that we'll sacrifice everything else to satisfy. The challenges of this life from our soil and the unsatisfied desires of our roots combine to form a worldview, and it is from this set of beliefs that our behaviors emerge.

For Reflection:

1. In what ways has your life made an impact? How do you seek to make a difference—or have you given up hope in your ability to do so? Explain.

2. Have you ever experienced rich community? What circumstances or life situations helped create depth in those relationships?

3. Do you believe that God's knowledge of you flows from love, not judgment? How do you react to the idea that he shares *every* thought?

4. How does our hope in Jesus change our perspective of what it means to live under God's gaze, and what God thinks about us?

DAY 5: THE SHOOTS

Let's recap: The seed of our sinful heart is planted in the soil of a fallen world. We try to find life from that soil through the roots of our desires, because we have lost our connection to our Creator. But apart from contentment in him, our desires are thwarted. We're left wanting more. This reality is coupled with the truth that life in the fallen world of our soil varies from disappointing to traumatic.

All these factors conspire together to form the "shoots" in our lives.

What comes up out of our ground is the worldview, or belief system, that's been formed and impacted by the above components. Because our hearts are fallen and estranged from God, we process life in a broken world without taking him into account. We make rebellious decisions and also live in a world where we are sinned against by others, sometimes in horrific ways. Even in a best-case scenario—raised in a warm, loving home by Christian parents in a good neighborhood, etc.—our desires are never fully satisfied to our timing or liking.

As a result, we begin to make conclusions about God, ourselves, others and the world. The diagram on the next page demonstrates how our desires morph into idols, which we'll sacrifice everything to obtain.

Again, all Christians live with both an official theology and a functional theology. Our official theology is the faith we publicly profess. We proclaim many things about God, and declare with the psalmist that his "steadfast love is better than life" (Psalm 63:3), but we live very differently.

Here's a small example: I believe God sees everything I do, that I have been entrusted as his steward with children to shepherd and raise to adulthood and spiritual maturity. I believe I will be accountable for every idle word I speak. Even more significantly, I believe that my joy and contentment in life are found in walking in step with the Spirit, faithfully living out my calling. But there are countless times when my desire for comfort, solitude, and tranquility trumps everything else. I believe those things will give me life. This becomes my functional theology and I throw out my official theology in an instant, willing to yell at my children in order to get what I crave most.

There are even more stark examples. After a prominent minister was exposed with a grievously duplicitous life, one journalist remarked that this

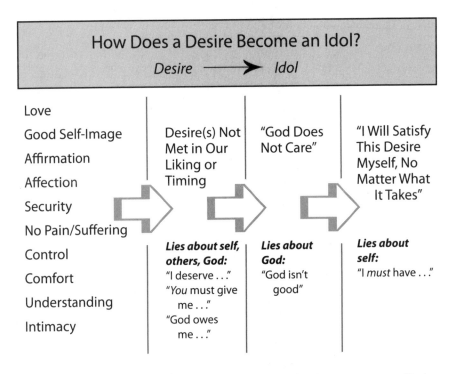

How Does a Desire Become an Idol?

Desire ——→ *Idol*

Love	Desire(s) Not Met in Our Liking or Timing	"God Does Not Care"	"I Will Satisfy This Desire Myself, No Matter What It Takes"
Good Self-Image			
Affirmation			
Affection			
Security			
No Pain/Suffering			
Control	*Lies about self, others, God:* "I deserve . . ." "*You* must give me . . ." "God owes me . . ."	*Lies about God:* "God isn't good"	*Lies about self:* "I *must* have . . ."
Comfort			
Understanding			
Intimacy			

person's entire ministry focused on telling people that Jesus was all they needed to be happy, yet apparently in his case he needed amphetamines and gay sex too.

We begin to draw conclusions from our life experience usually without even realizing we're doing it. Our functional theology is almost subconscious. This is why many of us have lived as Christians, even professing orthodox doctrines, yet have a private life that looks pagan. We draw conclusions about ourselves, others, the world, expectations of life, and especially God.

The latter is particularly important. Given our life experience, guilt and shame, and bad teaching, we come to radically unbiblical conclusions about God. We believe he is detached from our pain, or impotent to stop it. We see him as judge and taskmaster, or cosmic killjoy. Even as Christians, many of us live with deep-seated pockets of unbelief in our hearts, unwittingly believing lies about God.

Further, we believe lies about ourselves, others, and life in general. If we've never felt connection with our gender and have been called "queer" even before we understood its meaning, we conclude we must be gay. If we were treated like we never quite measured up as children, we might be driven to receive affirmation from others regardless of the cost. Praying without ceasing for years to be made straight can lead to the conclusions "God doesn't love me" or "He must have made me gay." Or, we can conclude that the only way to find excitement and fulfillment in life is when we're desired by a woman or engaged in the thrill of the hunt. Or, we can believe that we are worthless, throwaway people and that's why God allowed us to be abused, or conclude the only way to get someone's love and acceptance is through sex. We believe life will always be miserable, people will always let us down, and that we should just turn inward and escape the pain through whatever means available.

The decisions we make and the behaviors we pursue flow from our beliefs. True life change only comes as God changes our hearts and our beliefs are transformed as our relationship with him deepens. As our faith grows and our understanding of his work and power expands, change begins to take place in our lives. In the next four weeks, we'll establish the theology for change in the work of Christ. It is a slow process, learning to undo patterns of thinking and entrenched behaviors that have been in place sometimes for decades, but true transformation is possible. Nothing short of radical re-creation is in view in the gospel of Jesus Christ.

At the heart of the gospel is the hope that God does for us what we can't do for ourselves. Ezekiel 36:25–27 describes this amazing transformation: "I will sprinkle clean water on you, and you shall be clean from all your uncleannesses, and from all your idols I will cleanse you. And I will give you a new heart, and a new spirit I will put within you. And I will remove the heart of stone from your flesh and give you a heart of flesh. And I will put my Spirit within you, and cause you to walk in my statutes and be careful to obey my rules."

Through Jesus' death our guilt is washed away, and by his resurrection and the outpouring of his Spirit our hearts are changed. We have the grace to walk in obedience as never before. Prior to knowing Jesus, we had no choice but to continue living in rebellion. There was no real power for lasting change. Even if we overcame struggles in one area, it tended to make us proud and self-righteous, not humble and grateful. From the beginning, we've needed a heart transplant. In Jesus, God gives us a new heart, and his Spirit transforms our wayward beliefs and conforms our behavior to look like Christ's.

For Reflection:

1. What two or three life experiences cause (or could have caused) you to question God's goodness, love, or power?

2. Which past relationships have been the most painful? How do they continue to impact your ability to move toward others?

3. Where do you most find your identity—job, status, wife, salary, possessions? Why?

WEEK 4:
THE WAY TO THE PROMISED LAND

KEY CONCEPT: Israel was God's chosen people—not because of their performance, but because of God's love and mercy. Theirs is a history of repeated, stubborn, willful rebellion—just like ours. Having been delivered out of slavery in Egypt and brought into the Promised Land, they repeatedly chose idolatry over worship of the God who chose them. Eventually, they were conquered and expelled from the land—sent into exile as God had warned.

For many, this mirrors our experience of the Christian life. We were delivered from sin and folly, only to find ourselves slinking back, enslaved again. But the gospel is about more than going to heaven when we die! Central to Christ's mission was his commitment to deliver us from slavery and give us abundant life. He entered our exile, and endured its deepest depths, in order to conquer our greatest enemy and begin our glorious restoration.

DAY 1: IN THE BEGINNING . . .

Over the next couple weeks, we'll focus on how God has worked in human history. This is not a meaningless diversion from focusing on your struggle with sin. In fact, it is crucial that we connect our current struggles to the big picture of God's redemptive work. God's people have always struggled with obedience; therefore, it's helpful to see our similarities with them through the ages. More importantly, we need to observe God's ongoing commitment to his people, believing his faithfulness comes to rest on us just as it did with them.

Israel was a *chosen* people. Out of all the families of the earth, God put his favor on Abraham, calling him away from his hometown and sending him to the land of Canaan. They were also a *miraculous* people, as Abraham's wife gave birth to his son Isaac after decades of barrenness, when they were both well beyond normal childbearing age. Both were significant aspects of Israel's national identity, but the event that set Israel apart from all other nations happened hundreds of years later.

You probably know the story: Abraham's grandson Jacob moved the whole clan down to Egypt, when his son Joseph came to power and delivered the family from a multiyear famine engulfing the whole region. They lived in Egypt for 400 years, eventually becoming the Egyptians' slaves. In the midst of their bondage, Israel cried out to God and he heard them, sending Moses to be their deliverer. When Pharaoh refused to let the Israelites leave, God sent a series of plagues, each of them demonstrating his greatness over the various false gods of the Egyptians. After the final plague—the killing of all Egyptian firstborn—Pharaoh drove Israel away . . . only to change his mind. He pursued them into the wilderness, to the banks of the Red Sea. As the people are terrified, Moses makes this glorious declaration: "Fear not, stand firm, and see the salvation of the LORD, which he will work for you today. For the Egyptians whom you see today, you shall never see again. The LORD will fight for you, and you have only to be silent" (Exodus 14:13–14). More powerfully than ever before, God revealed himself as the warrior who fights for his people. He parted the Red Sea so Israel could cross over on dry ground, and then brought it crashing down on the heads of the Egyptians. In one sweeping action, God delivered his people and destroyed their enemies.

The Exodus forged the identity of Israel. They were the people of this glorious, all-powerful God who delivered them from slavery and conquered their oppressors. The Old Testament writers repeatedly refer to this event, to give hope and inspiration in the face of new oppressors and trials. Their hope was that the same God who delivered them from Egypt would again set them free.

It is crucial to see that in all this, God delivered Israel purely out of his love and mercy, not because of their worthiness. As they saw Egypt approaching, they quaked with fear: "Is it because there are no graves in Egypt that you have taken us away to die in the wilderness? What have you done to us in bringing us out of Egypt? Is not this what we said to you in Egypt: 'Leave us alone that we may serve the Egyptians'? For it would have been better for us to serve the Egyptians than to die in the wilderness" (Exodus 14:11–12). Israel was not delivered because of their great faith, but because of God's great love.

Most people know the story of the golden calf in Exodus 32, but Israel's rebellion goes even deeper. Ezekiel recounts that when God delivered them from Egypt, he told them to abandon their idols and forsake the gods of Egypt . . . and they refused! They chose to pack their idols for the trip to the Promised Land, but God acted "for the sake of [his] name" and still delivered them (see Ezekiel 20:4–10). For the sake of Christ, the Father continues to deal mercifully with us in the face of our continued rebellion, even as he invites us to see the infinitely greater blessings he wants to give us.

For Reflection:

1. As a Christian, you have experienced an exodus from the slavery of sin and death. How real does that fact seem to you? Explain.

2. Israel's identity was based upon the exodus. Where do you find your identity? Is it rooted in what Jesus has done for you, or in something else? (One way to think about this is: What do you want others to know about you? What's important for you to communicate about yourself when you first meet someone?)

3. What encouragement can you gain from the fact that Israel continued to rebel against God, even as he delivered them from Egypt?

DAY 2: THE ORIGIN OF EXILE

Israel's story doesn't end with the exodus and their conquest of the Promised Land. The other significant event in their history is their experience of exile. Let's enter into that experience.

The noon sun glares down on a long train of captives, slowly winding their way through the desert waste. It's a sweltering day. The sun beats down on their bent backs and radiates up from the sand, scorching their down-turned faces. The air between them is close. They feel the heat emanating from the other bodies packed alongside them as the line slowly trudges along. The sound of shuffling feet and clinking chains fills their ears.

Soldiers on horseback ride along the line, taunting and mocking. Their whips provide incentive to any who falter. Their horses are heavy-laden with the belongings of their captives. They gloat as they anticipate their arrival home with the plunder. Although the flame of their lust has been temporarily quenched by many who now stumble beside them, chained and weeping bitterly, the soldiers leer at the women, considering their options for when they hear the command to halt for the night.

The stench of sweat, blood, and human waste fills the air. Less penetrating, but far more painful, is the faint smell of distant smoke. The homes of the captives are going up in flames. The walls of their city have been pulled to the ground. The temple—the symbol of Israel's strength, the home of their God—has been desecrated, plundered, and engulfed in flame. When the fires die down, jackals will enter the city to feast on the corpses strewn about the streets. Already, vultures circle the smoldering ruins.

"Oh, the horrors of this day! I've lived as a member of Judah's nobility. Now everything I owned has been stripped from me. My wife was raped and killed before my eyes. My only child was mutilated beneath the trampling hooves of these uncircumcised pagans. The Babylonians forced our king to watch as his sons were brutally killed one after the other before his face. Then they gouged out his eyes, forever burning into his mind that final vision of his sons' bloody bodies, the complete destruction of his family, the utter end of his rule.

"I never thought it would come to this. Our priests assured us everything was fine, that God was with us. We had nothing to fear from Babylon. As the other nations were conquered one by one, we were convinced that God's favor rested on us. He had protected us from the Assyrians, even when the northern kingdom of Israel was destroyed.

"Of course, we weren't content with YHWH[6] alone. We sought the favor of all the gods. Over the years, our temple was filled with new gods to worship. Perhaps we diverged from our ancestors' religion, but we were progressive, learning to adapt and change with the times. Following the Law was so constricting. At the time, I thought it was great. Our feasts and festivals were extravagant. My escapades with the male and female temple prostitutes were incredible.

"In contrast, YHWH's prophets were pathetic. How we mocked them! They looked ridiculous, walking about in rags, standing on the street corner calling us to repent of our wickedness. They decried our modern worship. They were too uptight. How could sex *not* be central to worship? They wanted to keep our religion bland and esoteric. We wanted worship to be a glorious experience. We wanted gods we could see and feel. We thought we had it all.

"They warned us of the coming destruction, but the king's counselors shouted them down. They were imprisoned. Some were murdered. We thought we were immune to annihilation and could indulge our pleasures, with the blessing of all the gods. So their warnings went unheeded.

"Now, the memory of my temple revelry is bitter. I guess the prophets were right. Here we are shackled, led into captivity. Our king is childless, blinded and chained. Our temple, formerly a wonder to behold, is plundered and burned to the ground. The rest of our city is in flames. We have lost everything. And now we are fated to end our days as slaves in a foreign land. All is lost."

For Reflection:

1. How do you respond to Israel's experience of exile? Does it make you fearful? Do you think you should be afraid or not? Explain.

2. Does it seem unfair to you that God did this? Why or why not? How do you reconcile Israel's experience of God's wrath with your understanding of him through Jesus?

3. How is your experience of the Christian life similar to Israel's experience—which not only included the exodus from Egypt and conquest of Canaan, but also idolatry and exile?

DAY 3: EXILE DIDN'T START WITH YOU

One of this week's goals is to help you connect your life with the big picture—to see both the experience of God's people through the ages and his great redemptive work, which continues with you.

When Israel entered the Promised Land, God gave them stern warnings to avoid the inhabitants. They were actually commanded to commit genocide against the Canaanites, Amorites, Hittites—all the pagan people living in the land. Although it's hard for us to get our minds around this decree, God was concerned about protecting his people from the idols of the land. Those living in Canaan were involved in all kinds of heinous idolatrous practices, including regularly sacrificing their own children to their gods. Their cultures were marked by oppression and injustice.

God warned that if Israel allowed these nations to survive, they would begin to intermarry and before long Israel would abandon their covenant with God, choosing to worship the idols of the nations. God's purpose was to protect the purity of his people, through whom he was going to bring a deliverer. Despite his warnings, God knew they would rebel and predicted through Moses that it would happen with grievous results: Israel would be conquered by a pagan nation and driven out of the land. Before that, they would be besieged for years. Desperate and starving, they would even resort to eating their children (see Deuteronomy 28:53)!

Despite the eventual exile, God's dealings with Israel were filled with mercy. Given the fact that they left Egypt with idols in their luggage, made the golden calf while God was giving Moses the Ten Commandments, and repeatedly turned to worship idols throughout the periods of the judges and kings, God demonstrated incredible longsuffering. Even when he brought judgment, it was tempered with mercy. The ultimate goal was redemption, serving as an example of "looking in a mirror dimly" at the ultimate experience of exile by the only truly righteous Israelite, the Suffering Servant, Jesus.

God's people have a long, sordid history of abandoning him for other gods. In Week 2 we looked at Jeremiah's indictment of Israel's forsaking God, "the fountain of living water," to dig their own leaky cisterns. Jeremiah challenged the people about this reality right before the hammer was about to fall. But what is truly amazing is that God didn't leave them there. Just as he foretold the rebellion of Israel in Deuteronomy 28, so in Deuteronomy 30 God promised their restoration and his blessing upon them. This is where we are headed.

The exile is an important biblical theme for Christians struggling with sexual sin. I suspect there were sin areas in your life where God enabled you to experience victory when you came to faith in Jesus—perhaps substance abuse, gambling, certain forms of sexual sin, or cursing. You experienced a joyful sense of freedom from sin you never thought possible and assumed it would last the rest of your life. But then, old sins began to creep back in, or new sins gained ground in your life.

One colleague describes the experience of looking at porn and masturbating for the first time as a Christian man, after experiencing months of victory after his conversion. He was devastated. He felt in his soul, "It's baaaack . . . " His battle against lust didn't just magically disappear, as he'd hoped.

In the face of this, too many of us try to fight it alone. We reason that no one else in the church is talking about it, so why should we? We conclude we must be the only ones with a problem.

Fighting alone is impossible. And as we'll see later on, it's totally against God's design for our growth as Christians. When we fail repeatedly, the Christian life loses its luster. Our joy and zeal for the kingdom diminishes on two fronts. We feel like failures and hypocrites, but at the same time we delight in our sin even though it makes us miserable afterward.

From a spiritual standpoint, we end up in a very "exilic" place. We go from the joy of being delivered from sin's slavery and the zeal of experiencing victory as we grow in Christ, to feeling like a desperate and defeated failure, asking, "Is this all there is to the Christian life?"

For Reflection:

1. What was it like when you first believed in Jesus? How did it feel to know that your sins were forgiven, that you were free from the fear of death . . . that the Creator of the universe actually *cared* about you?

2. Did you experience initial freedom from your struggle with sexual sin when you came to faith? If so, when did the struggle begin to come back? How have you responded?

3. In what ways do you find yourself doubting God's power, love, and goodness because you're still facing these same old struggles? Explain.

DAY 4: JESUS' MISSION: RECONCILIATION AND RESTORATION

Over the next few weeks, we'll look more closely at the work of Christ, expose some of our common misconceptions, and examine God's plan of redemption for this world. The goal of the Christian life is not simply "you get to go to heaven when you die." Jesus invites us to begin eternal life *now*!

Listen to Jesus' definition: "And this is eternal life, that they know you the only true God, and Jesus Christ whom you have sent" (John 17:3). The purpose of Jesus' death and resurrection is to reconcile our broken relationships with God and others, to establish the kingdom of God, and ultimately renew the entire cosmos, including the creation of a new humanity of whom Jesus is the new Adam. So Paul writes, "He is the beginning, the firstborn from the dead, that in everything he might be preeminent" (Colossians 1:18b; see also Romans 5:12–21).

Restored relationship with God is at the center of the Christian life. Although many talk about a personal relationship with Jesus, many Christians don't have a vital, life-sustaining relationship with him. Unless we abide in Jesus, as a branch in a vine, we will not bear fruit and are in danger of being pruned. But as we abide in him, his life flows into us and bears much fruit (see John 15:1–11). There's a lot to abiding in Jesus—including resting and work, personal commitment and community support, a ruthless commitment to turn from our sin, and the ability to walk in honest, humble repentance where sin continues to dog us.

Further, the gospel heals our relationships. As we're moved by the grace of God and compelled by the love of Christ, we're able to lay down our lives for others. The more we learn the blessings of our relationship with Christ, the deeper our anticipation and hope will be in the life to come, and the more we'll find our life now by losing it for his sake.

John Lennon couldn't have gotten it more wrong in his song "Imagine." It is only when we live in certainty of the world to come that we're able to live as selflessly as he imagines we should. As we'll see in the weeks to come, our relationships are increasingly transformed as we live openly and honestly, trusting in God's goodness, willing to be known by others and—taking our eyes off ourselves—desiring to know them more deeply.

In Luke 4:14–30, we see Jesus begin his earthly ministry by publicly reading from Isaiah 61. Listen to the calling given to him by the Father:

The Spirit of the Lord God is upon me,
  because the Lord has anointed me
to bring good news to the poor;
  he has sent me to bind up the brokenhearted,
to proclaim liberty to the captives,
  and the opening of the prison to those who are bound;
to proclaim the year of the Lord's favor,
  and the day of vengeance of our God;
  to comfort all who mourn;
to grant to those who mourn in Zion—
to give them a beautiful headdress instead of ashes,
  the oil of gladness instead of mourning,
  the garment of praise instead of a faint spirit;
  that they may be called oaks of righteousness,
  the planting of the Lord, that he may be glorified
They shall build up the ancient ruins;
  they shall raise up the former devastations;
they shall repair the ruined cities,
  the devastations of many generations. (Isaiah 61:1–4)

Here's the bottom line: The work of Christ is to overturn the effects of the curse. He came to free us from the heartache and pain of life in a fallen world. He came to deliver us from our slavery to sin. And again, his ultimate mission is to renew the entire cosmos. Notice that the promise of what will happen in and through us flows from *his* work. Isaiah draws from the language of exile: God would restore his people to the Promised Land, devastated by the ravages of war and oppression by pagan nations, and empower them to bring renewal to that broken place. Likewise, God calls us to be his ambassadors, to have a significant role in establishing and extending his kingdom, even as we await Christ's final return and the consummation of all his promises.

Throughout all of redemptive history, even in the midst of severe discipline, God always reveals that he is characterized by mercy. Consider the following words from the letter written through Jeremiah to those living in exile:

For thus says the Lord: When seventy years are completed for
Babylon, I will visit you, and I will fulfill to you my promise and

bring you back to this place. For I know the plans I have for you, declares the LORD, plans for wholeness and not for evil, to give you a future and a hope. Then you will call upon me and come and pray to me, and I will hear you. You will seek me and find me. When you seek me with all your heart, I will be found by you, declares the LORD, and I will restore your fortunes and gather you from all the nations and all the places where I have driven you, declares the LORD, and I will bring you back to the place from which I sent you into exile. (Jeremiah 29:10–14)

It is truly astounding that in the face of Israel's rebellion, God continues to show love and mercy! His plan had always been to bless them, despite their sin. And he is committed to showing compassion and grace to us, in spite of ourselves!

For Reflection:

1. How has God disciplined you? What consequences have you faced because of your sin? How has God intervened to expose your sin despite your attempts to keep it hidden? Where do you see his love in all this?

2. How have you experienced God's mercy? In what ways have you not received what you deserved?

3. How does Christ's description of his mission in Isaiah 61 fit with your understanding of the Christian life? How does it change it?

DAY 5: THE END OF EXILE

When did the exile end? How did God restore his people? There is a striking passage in Ezra 3 recounting the rebuilding of the temple. Babylon received her payback, just as God promised, and was conquered by the Persians. After the time set by God, the Jews found favor with King Cyrus of Persia and were allowed to return to the land and rebuild Jerusalem, including the temple. This should have been a cause of great celebration, right? But listen to Ezra's account:

> And all the people shouted with a great shout when they praised the
> LORD, because the foundation of the house of the LORD was laid.
> But many of the priests and Levites and heads of fathers' houses, old
> men who had seen the first house, wept with a loud voice when they
> saw the foundation of this house being laid, though many shouted
> aloud for joy, so that the people could not distinguish the sound
> of the joyful shout from the sound of the people's weeping, for the
> people shouted with a great shout, and the sound was heard far
> away. (Ezra 3:11b–13)

The younger generation celebrated, but the older generation—those who experienced Israel's previous glory—*wept*! Something was very wrong. This was not the restoration they anticipated; this was not what the prophets promised. The only reason they were even there is because Cyrus allowed it. They weren't free from their pagan overlords, the promises hadn't been fulfilled, and they knew it. Sure, more Jews returned to the land over the following centuries. By the time of Jesus they had even rebuilt the temple. Perhaps the furnishings weren't as lavish as the former temple, but the new structure was at least on a grander scale.

But something was still very wrong: from the time of the Babylonian exile in the sixth century BC until the creation of the modern political state of Israel in 1948, the Jews lived under the thumb of pagan rulers. After the Babylonians came the Persians, then the Greeks, then the Romans. Though back in the land, the Jews were still experiencing the pain of exile. God's people continued to suffer oppression—waiting for God to intervene, free them from the uncircumcised pagans and their detestable practices, and usher in all the promises he had made through his prophets. That's how the Old Testament ends.

Then, in the fullness of time, Jesus entered the world. The true King arrived at last. But he was not what they expected. "He came to his own, and his own people did not receive him" (John 1:11). He was born to peasants. His very conception was radically misunderstood, likely met with sneering and raised eyebrows throughout his life (see John 8:41 for one example). Yet he walked through the world spreading life and light wherever he placed his feet. His miracles demonstrated his kingship and the reality that his kingdom had come. As the hymn "Joy to the World" captures so well, "He comes to make his blessings flow. Far as the curse is found." Jesus' ministry was a powerful demonstration of the curse being overturned, the renewal and restoration of a dying world.

But his work didn't stop there. He was seized by his enemies, subjected to a farcical trial, and sentenced to die a brutally painful and shameful death. He was condemned for claiming to be God. Thus, in a very literal sense, he was punished specifically for *our* crime. As discussed in Week 2, our sexual sin reveals our yearning to be God, to create a world in which we are at the center and everything revolves around our satisfaction, our glory. In stark contrast, Jesus *is* God! He is the only human who could ever truly make that claim, although every other person in the history of the world has lived as if it were true of him or her.

But the mind-boggling reality is that it was all God's plan. Peter, in his great sermon at Pentecost, declares: "[T]his Jesus, *delivered up according to the definite plan and foreknowledge of God*, you crucified and killed by the hands of lawless men" (Acts 2:23, emphasis added). Jesus willingly entered our exile.

When the Jews returned from their captivity in Babylon, they knew they were still oppressed, the exile wasn't over. Here's the truth: The exile reached its deepest, most horrific depth when the true King of Israel was cruelly mocked, beaten to a bloody pulp, marched outside the city into the wilderness, stripped naked and lifted up to be slaughtered. Fulfilling the Old Testament prophecies concerning the day of the Lord (see Joel 2 in particular), the sun was blotted out as the Lord of glory was killed by pagan forces and the armies of darkness. Now the exile was complete, and the promises of God about to be unleashed . . . [7]

Jesus' followers scattered in dismay. They feared all was lost, but could not have been more deeply mistaken! The exile was finally over and Jesus rose victorious on Easter morning, the conqueror of sin and death. Through the cross, "[h]e disarmed the rulers and authorities and put them to open shame" (Colossians 2:15). He "was declared to be the Son of God in power according to the Spirit of holiness by his resurrection" (Romans 1:4). He is now reigning over this universe, upholding all things by the "word of his power" (Hebrews 1:3). The resurrection is the proof that he "was heard because of his reverence" (Hebrews 5:7), and that in him all the promises of God are fulfilled. As firstborn from the dead, he is the beginning of God's great work of re-creation!

Jesus has suffered the punishment of exile for you, and now offers you the power of his indestructible life. The Christian life is not pie-in-the-sky, where eventually you'll get to heaven, but the radical intervention of a loving God to redeem this broken world and bring his people to glory! He promises to restore your sexual sanity.

For Reflection:

1. List some specific activities in your life that reflect "exile living." Are you willing to leave that exile and return to the Promised Land? If not, what holds you back?

2. If you've never understood your need for forgiveness and cried out to God for mercy, I pray your heart will be stirred as you consider Jesus' sacrifice for you. Will you ask him for forgiveness and to fill you with his Spirit, giving you resurrection power to live differently?

3. If you've already trusted your life to Christ, where do you need to repent and return to your King? If you entered the Christian life with joy years ago and have grown disenchanted due to the trials and temptations of this life, are you ready to get up and get back in the race? List a few specific ramifications of this decision. What would this renewed allegiance to God look like in your life? What positive changes need to take place?

SECTION 2:
THE CONQUERING KING

WEEK 5:
THE DELIVERER

KEY CONCEPT: There are many skewed views of Jesus, but these misconceptions tend to fall into one of two categories. Quite often, Jesus is pictured as purely tender and gentle, with a lamb draped over his shoulders or a child on his knee. However, some corners of the church, put off by an effeminate Jesus, try instead to "masculinize" him—creating a Jesus for "real men." Both these caricatures miss the essence of the gospel.

Jesus has strength radically different from our own. He came to deliver us from sin and death, establishing the kingdom of God in this broken world. In his death, Jesus was victorious because he endured the curse of the covenant in order to unleash its blessings. Through Jesus' resurrection, ascension, and the outpouring of his Spirit, God offers us genuine life change here and now. Because of the incarnation, Jesus understands our experience, knows how much grace we need to obey, and gives his Spirit to empower us.

DAY 1: HE'S *NOT* WHO YOU THINK . . .

Depending on your age, if you were raised in the church you probably have memories of sitting bored in Sunday school while the teacher moved little cloth images of Jesus, the disciples, Pharisees and tax collectors around the flannelgraph. The Jesus of children's Bibles is handsome, maybe a little effeminate, with a lamb draped over his shoulders or children on his knee. Contemporary pop-culture has taken up the theme, with James Caviezel playing an attractive, improbably blue-eyed Jesus in *The Passion of the Christ* as opposed to the prophetic description, "He had no form or majesty that we should look at him, and no beauty that we should desire him" (Isaiah 53:2b).

Church culture gives the picture of a Jesus who's gentle, mild-mannered, and well-behaved.

Sadly, our theology often mirrors these wrong perceptions. Much of American Christianity sees Jesus as the "cosmic savior guy" who allowed himself to be mocked, beaten and killed for our sins—characterized more by weakness than strength. Perhaps we've read accounts of the horrors of crucifixion and have a sense of gratitude for his suffering, but still we see him primarily as coming to die. "Savior" is diminished to "the one who came to die for me."

This is a Jesus that most of us have trouble relating to. We're aware in some sense that through Jesus' sacrifice our sins are atoned for, and we're grateful for that. We're thankful that God has forgiven us and promises that we won't go to hell when we die. But in this life, Jesus' death doesn't seem to impact anything. And of course, ongoing struggles and repeated failures with sexual sin make the cross appear even more irrelevant to our daily life, allegedly promising a victory we haven't experienced.

In response to the flannelgraph picture of a weak, effeminate Jesus, there's a movement to portray Christ differently, recasting him as the quintessential "man's man"—Arnold Schwarzenegger in first-century peasant garb. Touting that he had calloused hands and big biceps, they make much of his clearing of the temple. In the words of one author, in order to give the church's view of Jesus a healthy shot of testosterone they picture "The Ultimate Fighting Jesus"—a Jesus that "real men" can look up to and emulate.[8]

But here's the rub: These people are simply creating Jesus in their own image, making significant assumptions that certain aspects of maleness are God-given—our tendency toward self-sufficiency, our aggression, our avoidance of emotions. In reality, clinging to these aspects of your maleness also keeps you chained to your sexual sin. We need to be extremely wary in our portrayals of Jesus, particularly if the image reminds you of who you already see when you look in the mirror.

For Reflection:

1. When have you encountered the caricature of the flannelgraph Jesus? How does it impact your faith to think of Jesus solely as "the one who came to die"?

2. Have you been attracted to "The Ultimate Fighting Jesus"? What makes this view of Christ more attractive?

3. How does what you know of Jesus from the Gospels challenge both of these perspectives?

DAY 2: JESUS CONFORMED TO *OUR* IMAGE?

Both the extremes described yesterday give a distorted view of Jesus that reveals our hearts. Remaking Jesus in the image of Western culture's masculine ideal whitewashes many of our sinful male tendencies. It creates a Jesus who simply baptizes our maleness as it is, not one who radically reshapes it. Ultimately, this Jesus won't demand much from us, because there isn't much that needs to be changed.

One group asserts that men should be "Boss, Bold, Brash, Bully, and Blunt."[9] What are they saying? In essence: "I can stay arrogant, competitive, obnoxious, and crass, because that's who God made me to be." The proponents of this viewpoint argue that conversion doesn't take away this essential "maleness," despite the fact that the Bible explicitly says those who are in Christ will have lives that look radically different than who we are naturally. Consider this example: "Put on then, as God's chosen ones, holy and beloved, compassion, kindness, humility, meekness, and patience. . . . " (Colossians 3:12). Clearly, these are two radically opposed worldviews.

Now, this doesn't mean men can't relate to one another through busting on each other, or trash-talking on the basketball court. But our interactions need to go deeper than that. We don't have to sit around and talk about feelings every time we're hanging out to watch a game, but there are times when we need to get real with brothers about what's going on in our souls. Part of the lie we believe is that it's somehow unmasculine to experience emotions, so we stuff them. Consider David and Jonathan weeping at their parting, Jesus weeping over Jerusalem, the elders of various churches in Acts weeping as they bid farewell to Paul. David the giant killer, who slaughtered two hundred Philistines and presented their foreskins to win the hand of Saul's daughter, a leader so revered his men risked their lives just to fetch him a cup of water from his favorite well in enemy-held territory—this warrior-king was also a poet and musician, in touch with his emotions. He even danced in the modern equivalent of his underwear before the ark as it was brought into Jerusalem.

I'm concerned less with how we relate to one another, and more particularly with how we engage women and children, including our sons. The harsh ways that we tend to relate to each other just don't fit. Consider the calling from 1 Peter 3:7, "Likewise, husbands, live with your wives in an understanding way, showing honor to the woman as the weaker vessel. . . ." Scripture is not making men superior by describing women as weaker. It's saying they were created to be softer, gentler, and needing to be tenderly cared for with consideration and honor. This care enables them to flourish. There may well be times you need to be "Boss, Bold, Brash, Bully, and Blunt" to protect those dearest to you in a fallen world, but your personal interactions with them should look very different.

Other men struggle with typical male forms of relating, and we need to be aware of that too. There is a whole spectrum of personality and gifting that God created and declares male. We need to understand how our perspective of maleness is often more culturally conditioned than biblically instructed. This particularly applies if you have a son who is more tenderhearted than you'd like. Forcing him to put worms on the fish hook, or berating him for crying when he's hurt will make him feel all the more estranged from you and maleness in general. You need wisdom to affirm him as male and prepare him for what that means in covering and protecting those who are weaker, but celebrate how God has made him— even if that means you're going to violin recitals instead of Little League games.

Jesus doesn't call men to become a bunch of sissies, but to a strength that's radically different than they had before conversion. This strength doesn't win barroom brawls, but it faces and conquers the evil and injustice in this world, often through crushing self-sacrifice. This is real strength. This is what it means to be a godly, mighty man.

The feminized Jesus doesn't challenge us either. It makes it easier to minimize our sins—if he already died for them, we don't need to take them terribly seriously. After all, we're under grace! Further, because our focus tends to be on the hereafter— we get to go to heaven when we die!—it doesn't seem like Jesus is offering any real change in the here and now. Therefore, again, he can't expect much from us. We might have some ability to grow on our own, and we do feel guilty about our sin—especially when we've really gone overboard—but there's no real hope for significant lifelong change. The view of "Jesus meek and mild" can also feed men's struggle with passivity. We shirk the places God calls us to be courageous by hiding behind false humility and timidity, all the while calling it gentleness.

Most of us need to reverse our natural tendencies. In the places where we typically demonstrate "strength"—perhaps ruling over your family with an iron fist—we need greater gentleness, kindness, humility, concern for the needs of our wives and children. We need to become great leaders by being the servant of all. Where we tend to shrink back—engaging the hearts of family members, helping them process life, leading them spiritually—we need to show much greater courage and strength. As we'll see, in both these things we are utterly dependent on God to bring about the necessary changes.

For Reflection:

1. Have you struggled with "cheap grace"—the idea that because Jesus died for your sins past, present, and future, you don't need to sweat it? Has anyone—spouse, friends, parents—ever challenged that view in you?

2. How do you interact with women and children? In what ways do you need to change in relating to your wife as the "weaker vessel"? Where are you in danger of frustrating or exasperating your children (see Ephesians 6:4 and Colossians 3:21)? Do you have the courage to ask them these questions and really listen?

3. How does the Jesus of the Gospels challenge our natural maleness? Where is he calling you to be bold? Where do you need to grow in humility?

DAY 3: NOT "SAVIOR"—DELIVERER

When the average American Christian hears Jesus described as Savior, the fact that he died for my sins immediately comes to mind. Saving is seen as synonymous with dying. But something much deeper and richer is actually in view. Jesus' atoning sacrifice is utterly central to our faith, but we need to deepen our understanding of what that means for us and how that truth is meant to transform our lives, *today*.

Jesus' very name communicates this more radical meaning. It is a Greek pronunciation of the Hebrew name *Yeshua* (or Joshua in English). It means "YHWH delivers!" Last week, we read how the Jews were still living in exile, oppressed by pagan overlords even though they had returned to the Promised Land. They longed for deliverance. They were seeking a messiah who would be the new Moses, delivering them from the bondage of foreign oppression, restoring sovereign rule of the Promised Land to the chosen people. The Hebrew word *messiah* in fact means "anointed one" and refers to a formal, kingly office. Therefore, the Jews were looking for the son of David who would lead them in battle against the pagan forces. They wanted real, here-and-now deliverance.

Many Christians don't realize that Christ is a formal title, the Greek word for *messiah*. It would be more accurate to refer to Jesus as "*the* Christ." It is a declaration of his kingship. Jesus was and is the expected son of David—but his method of deliverance looked radically different, and was infinitely greater, than any Jew of the first century had ever imagined.

We need to think about salvation differently. A fireman puts his life on the line when he rushes into the flames to save a terrified child, but his goal is not to identify with the child in death. Saving does not mean surrendering with the child to the inferno, but rescuing him from the blaze and returning him to his anxious mother's arms. A commando doesn't enter a terrorist stronghold in order to be kidnapped along with the other hostages. He puts his life on the line to deliver them from death. If he takes a bullet, it's so they won't.

In the same way, Jesus' sacrificial death was not merely a way to identify with us under the curse, to bring about some eventual, otherworldly existence when we die. We do need deliverance from our eternal punishment, but we also need deliverance from our slavery to sin right here and now. Jesus drank the cup of God's wrath to its dregs so that we would know freedom *today*. He did not go to the cross only to deliver us from the literal hell awaiting the enemies of God; he also saves us from the hell we create for ourselves and those we love through our sinful behavior.

A savior is worthy of the name only if the people he saves are actually delivered from their bondage. The Greek word *soter*, usually translated "savior," might be better understood as "deliverer." More than simply coming to die, Jesus' mission was to redeem us, to buy us back. But to understand this reality, we'll need to go back even further in the history of redemption . . .

For Reflection:

1. When you think of Jesus as Savior, do you tend to focus more on otherworldly (heavenly) ideas? What does his sacrifice mean to you beyond "you get to go to heaven when you die"?

2. The Jews of Jesus' day expected their deliverance to look differently. What are your own expectations of deliverance? In what ways might they need to be changed?

3. How have your former attempts to overcome sexual sin diminished your understanding of Jesus' work of deliverance? Do you still believe victory over your sin is possible? Why or why not?

DAY 4: THE COVENANT FULFILLED

When Adam and Eve rebelled against God, they became enslaved to sin and death. By their own choosing, they willingly became subjects of Satan and his domain of darkness. They entered spiritual exile, and the physical world was accursed. However, the story didn't end there. When God pronounced judgment at the fall, he also promised to send a *soter*—a deliverer to crush the head of their oppressor and free his people (see Genesis 3:15).

A perhaps lesser-known story comes from the time God promised that *he* would be the deliverer, specifically by personally paying the price. He would redeem—buy back—his people, and deliver on his promise by literally taking the curse of the fall on himself.

Genesis 15 recounts God's covenant with Abraham. He called Abraham to go through a ritual that sounds very strange to our 21st-century ears. Abraham sacrificed a heifer, a goat, a ram, a turtledove, and a pigeon, cutting the bigger animals in half and arranging the pieces across from one another, to form a narrow path between them. Although seemingly bizarre to us, Abraham knew exactly what was happening. This was a regular ritual in the ancient Near East, called a suzerain-vassal treaty. When a greater tribal king conquered a lesser king and promised to spare his life, the lesser king would go through this ritual. It was a way of showing gratitude and absolute loyalty. The lesser king would "pass through the pieces," promising to serve the victor and submitting to the consequences if he rebelled. He was saying, in effect, "May I be torn in two like these animals if I fail in my promised allegiance to you." The conquered king was making a promise of such magnitude that he took a curse on himself if he betrayed it.

But something radical happened in God's ritual with Abraham. Who would you expect to pass through the pieces? It should have been Abraham, the lesser subject of the greater. God promised to bless and provide for him, to give him offspring as numerous as the stars. Abraham should be expected to offer complete allegiance to God and be cursed if the covenant was broken. But God does something amazingly different— appearing as a flaming torch and smoking fire pot, *he* passes through the pieces! So, God both gives the promises of blessing and takes the curse of the covenant on himself. The entire covenant is his responsibility. He promises to be "torn asunder" in order to fulfill the promise to be our God. He would deliver in a way completely unexpected and radically countercultural.

This is exactly what happens at the cross of Christ. As Jesus hangs dying, estranged from the Father, he cries out, "My God, my God—why have you forsaken me?" In a literal fulfillment of Genesis 15, the Godhead is "torn asunder," as the communion of Father and Son with the Spirit that existed from all eternity is broken. Jesus hangs dying under the curse, as Scripture declared, "Cursed is everyone who is hanged on a tree" (Galatians 3:13).

Our sin, and the brokenness of this world, made it impossible for a holy God to keep his covenant promise to be our God. Only the curse of the covenant could balance the equation. Jesus is the *soter*, the deliverer who came to undo the power of sin and death, conquering the forces of darkness and establishing God's victory in this broken world. In his death, Jesus emptied the covenant of its curse, so the blessing of God's promises might be poured out on his people. Look at how the Bible describes Jesus' work on the cross:

> And you, who were dead in your trespasses and the uncircumcision of your flesh, God made alive together with him, having forgiven us all our trespasses, by canceling the record of debt that stood against us with its legal demands. This he set aside, nailing it to the cross. He disarmed the rulers and authorities and put them to open shame, by triumphing over them in him. (Colossians 2:13–15)

> He is the radiance of the glory of God and the exact imprint of his nature, and he upholds the universe by the word of his power. After making purification for sins, he sat down at the right hand of the Majesty on high, having become as much superior to angels as the name he has inherited is more excellent than theirs. (Hebrews 1:3–4)

Jesus triumphed at the cross, defeating Satan's kingdom and delivering us from the guilt of our sin through his atoning sacrifice. The proof of his victory is the resurrection. The power of death is broken.

Further, the description of Jesus sitting at the right hand of God is crammed with meaning. He is given the place of ultimate power and authority, and he is seated because his work is complete! It is the picture of a victorious King, ruling over all things, having vanquished all his enemies. Paul encourages believers with the power that is theirs in Christ, by describing what Jesus accomplished through the cross and resurrection:

> And what is the immeasurable greatness of [God's] power toward us who believe, according to the working of his great might that he worked in Christ when he raised him from the dead and seated him at his right hand in the heavenly places, far above all rule and authority and power and dominion, and above every name that is named, not only in this age but also in the one to come. And he put all things under his feet and gave him as head over all things to the church, which is his body, the fullness of him who fills all in all. (Ephesians 1:19–23)

Our deliverance in Christ is not only the guarantee that we'll get to heaven, but the promise that the same power the Father exerted in raising Jesus from the dead is at work in us through his Spirit, to bring radical change to our lives even now. God's promise is not that you'll be delivered eventually. He is promising you deliverance *now* in Jesus because the curse is broken and emptied of power. Jesus is reigning over all things *now*, for the good of his church!

For Reflection:

1. How does it encourage you to know that God is completely responsible for every aspect of the covenant? What would it look like for you to believe that, and to rest in the work of Christ?

2. How does the idea of Jesus as deliverer change your perspective on his relevance to your life right now? How would your life be different if you fully believed that?

3. Where do you need to experience deliverance in your life—an exodus from slavery to sin? What would be different if Jesus brought you out of exile and back into the Promised Land?

DAY 5: THE RADICAL KING

At the cross, Jesus absorbed all the evil this broken world could muster. The full weight of the Roman Empire was thrown against him, spurred on by the unseen rulers and authorities in the spiritual realm (see Ephesians 6:10–20). The cross is not the picture of a weak, meek, and mild Jesus. When Peter chopped off the servant's ear in the garden of Gethsemane, do you remember Jesus' response? "Put your sword back into its place. For all who take the sword will perish by the sword. Do you think that I cannot appeal to my Father, and he will at once send me more than twelve legions of angels?" (Matthew 26:52–53). In a profound demonstration of strength, Jesus allowed himself to be crushed. By taking our punishment, Jesus defeated the power of Satan. And he demonstrated how the kingdom of God moves forward in this world—not by brute force, but in love; not by might, but through self-sacrificing individuals, empowered by the Spirit of God to take the message of hope and reconciliation under the true King, to a world enslaved by sin, misery, exploitation, and death.

Jesus' resurrection marks his coronation as the King. He rose victorious from the grave and established a new humanity (see 1 Corinthians 15:42–49). His followers would be those who lived not for themselves, but for him who died for them and was raised again (see 2 Corinthians 5:15). They would follow his radical countercultural teaching, showing mercy to the desperate and extending love to their enemies.

Jesus' deliverance frees us from slavery to sin, creating an army for God's kingdom. For those who swear allegiance to this King, there is freedom from the former tyrant. Jesus cancelled the record of debt that stood against us (Colossians 2:14). We are able to live in a reconciled relationship to God, which means his power is available to us. That is what the Bible promises—the power that raised Jesus from the dead is at work in us (see Romans 8:11 and Ephesians 1:19–21; 3:20–21). It's about living a life of freedom now. Jesus' power is real—and it is offered to you. Jesus is our reigning King. The cross, the resurrection, and the outpouring of the Spirit mean we can be delivered now from slavery to sin. Jesus is our deliverer who brings us out of the exile of our sexual sin. God offers you sexual sanity, and so much more.

Further, we are not left to accomplish this on our own. Jesus pours out his Spirit on us, enabling us to obey. The same Spirit that empowered Samson to slay a thousand men with a donkey's jawbone gives us spiritual power over sin. Actually, in Jesus we have even greater power than Samson, who remained a slave to his sexual desires.[10] Because the Spirit has been poured out, we have the hope of walking in obedience. God brings about in us, through his Spirit, what is impossible on our own. He knows the desperate straits we're in and promises to give us what we need.

Listen: We don't even know how to *pray* right! "Likewise the Spirit helps us in our weakness. For we do not know what to pray for as we ought, but the Spirit himself intercedes for us with groanings too deep for words" (Romans 8:26). And, as our Great High Priest, Jesus continues to minister to us. Hebrews 7:25 says, "Consequently, he is able to save to the uttermost those who draw near to God through him, since he always lives to make intercession for them." Jesus is able to deliver us completely because, through his resurrection, he lives forever interceding for his people, along with the groaning of the Spirit "too deep for words."

This is not abstract theology. Because Jesus came in the flesh, he knows exactly what we need. He is able to deliver us from sexual sin because he knows our struggles specifically. "Therefore he had to be made like his brothers in every respect, so that he might become a merciful and faithful high priest in the service of God, to make propitiation for the sins of the people. For because he himself has suffered when tempted, he is able to help those who are being tempted" (Hebrews 2:17–18). How was he tempted? Lest you think his experience was different than yours, we read elsewhere in Hebrews, "For we do not have a high priest who is unable to sympathize with our weaknesses, but one who in every respect has been tempted as we are, yet without sin" (Hebrews 4:15).

Listen to that hope. Jesus suffered the same temptations you experience. However, unlike other men who might empathize because they have the same weakness, but for that very reason are unable to offer real help, Jesus suffered in the exact same way—victoriously! He can give you the strength you need because he knows exactly what it takes, having endured the same temptations, without failing. He knows the grace you need to stand up under your temptation; that's why we are always promised a way out (see 1 Corinthians 10:13).

Jesus does not abandon you in your sin. He does not leave it up to you to become a good boy, now that you're saved. He is a deliverer from sin because he continues to work in us through his Spirit to bring transformation. Jesus promised, "I will not leave you as orphans; I will come to you" (John 14:18).

If we're honest with ourselves, we deal with fear. We often feel like orphans all alone in a big world and we're scared. Some fears are about the future, such as health or finances. We hide behind the "Boss, Bold, Brash, Bully, and Blunt" façade, but it's just a fig leaf—dried and falling apart in the wasteland heat. We fear exposure! Maybe outwardly you have it all together, but your biggest fear is having the sexual side of your life laid bare. Our fears keep us in chains. Jesus came to break those chains by creating a humanity known not by individual accomplishments, but by its identity with him as their King. We'll look more closely at what this means over the next two weeks.

For Reflection:

1. Do you believe you're stronger than Samson? Why or why not? Have you ever experienced this kind of strength? What was it like?

2. In what contexts are you most prone to posture and pretend like everything's fine? What does it look like when you do?

3. Are there places in life where you feel like an orphan? What would it be like to live in the knowledge that you're not alone?

WEEK 6:
THE REIGNING KING

KEY CONCEPT: Repeated failure with sexual sin causes many men to live in despair, feeling hopeless that victory over sin is even possible. The Bible makes sense of this experience, describing this world as under a curse, ruled by an enemy bent on misery and destruction. But the point of the gospel is that Jesus came to defeat the usurper and reestablish God's kingdom in this world. His kingdom is about overturning the effects of the curse, in both the physical and spiritual realms.

Following his resurrection and ascension, Jesus is described throughout the New Testament as the ruler of the universe. He is sovereign over all things, even if it doesn't *look* that way in the moment. Further, the Spirit is poured out to unite us with Christ and empower us to grow in ways that are impossible in our own strength—including the strength to overcome struggles with sin that have plagued us for decades.

DAY 1: REMEMBER—THEOLOGY MATTERS!

Are you becoming frustrated with all the focus on theology here? You want practical answers—the how-to's that will enable you to have victory over sexual sin. But our theology matters, because what we believe dramatically impacts how we live. Although developing new habits and holy responses to life in a fallen world are vitally important, ultimately our victory is not found in handy strategies. What we believe, and knowing how to apply our beliefs, determines whether we'll overcome our struggle with sin.

One man described his struggle with sexual sin this way: In college he owned a boa constrictor. Feeding time was always a big hit in the dormitory. The men would cordon off the area, place his snake in the center of the room, then drop in the mouse. The mouse was immediately aware of the danger and frantically dashed around the perimeter, desperately seeking a way of escape. The snake just sat patiently, almost disinterested, its tongue slowly flicking in and out. When the mouse realized there was no way out, he gave up and stood trembling before the snake, waiting for the end to come. The man articulated that in his battle against lust, he is that mouse. There is no escape; it's only a matter of time until the snake strikes. He is a helpless victim of an appetite he is powerless to control.

Another man who leads an accountability group said he and all of his men are mired in addiction to Internet pornography. He feels like all of them are in quicksand—covered with muck, slowly sinking to their doom. They've been stuck in their sin for so long that it seems impossible they'll ever get out. It will slowly get worse and worse until eventually they die in their sin.

Although they might not appear that way, both of these views are deeply theological, crammed with lies about the reality of their existence. Their shoots (see Week 3) are exposed. Unknowingly, they've drawn radically unbiblical conclusions about God, his power in redemption, and the hope they have in this life. Often we feel like our experience, especially our repeated failure with sexual sin, contradicts the teaching of Scripture. A counselor once shared that the experience of grief is like being in a dark basement on a beautiful sunny day. Our experience with guilt is similar—it doesn't negate the truth, but it clouds our ability to see it clearly. God's truth is discarded and our feelings and experiences become the ultimate authorities on reality.

This is radically counter to how God calls us to live. We are called to "walk by faith, not by sight" (2 Corinthians 5:7)—not interpreting life by our experiences and feelings, but according to God's promises. As we saw last week, the promise goes all the way back to the garden of Eden—that One was coming who would crush the head of the serpent. We are never left alone to tremble before our adversary. Jesus is our champion, who fights for us. He is our deliverer! Further, we are not left to drown in our sin. Jesus is the Rock, the foundation beneath our feet. In Christ, we belong to a kingdom that can't be shaken (Hebrews 12:28)! We are on solid ground.

I hope you're beginning to see how much our "functional theology" matters. It affects how we approach our struggle with sin. What we believe about our situations impacts how we'll respond to them.

For Reflection:

1. What lies do you believe about your struggle with sin? Does ongoing victory over temptation seem impossible? Do you believe it's only a matter of time before you fall again? Explain.

2. How has your experience negatively informed your understanding of what's ultimately true?

3. How do your conclusions dictate the outcome of your struggle against sin? What connections can you see between your functional theology and your behavior?

DAY 2: JESUS ESTABLISHED A KINGDOM

One of the most important questions we need to ask ourselves is: What did Jesus truly come to earth to do? What was his mission? Jesus declared repeatedly that in him the kingdom of God had come. He came to establish the kingdom of God. Although this refrain is regularly repeated throughout the Gospels, he made it explicit when challenged by the Pharisees in Matthew 12:22–30:

> Then a demon-oppressed man who was blind and mute was brought
> to him, and he healed him, so that the man spoke and saw. And all
> the people were amazed, and said, "Can this be the Son of David?"
> But when the Pharisees heard it, they said, "It is only by Beelzebul, the
> prince of demons, that this man casts out demons." Knowing their
> thoughts, he said to them, "Every kingdom divided against itself is
> laid waste, and no city or house divided against itself will stand. And if
> Satan casts out Satan, he is divided against himself. How then will his
> kingdom stand? And if I cast out demons by Beelzebul, by whom do
> your sons cast them out? Therefore they will be your judges. But if it is
> by the Spirit of God that I cast out demons, then the kingdom of God
> has come upon you. Or how can someone enter a strong man's house
> and plunder his goods, unless he first binds the strong man? Then
> indeed he may plunder his house. Whoever is not with me is against
> me, and whoever does not gather with me scatters."

Do you hear the people's anticipation? Seeing Jesus' power over demons and physical infirmity, they ask, "Can this be the son of David?" They are expressing their hope that a new King would arrive to deliver them from their enemies. Jesus' point was clear: he cast out demons by the Spirit of God, as a demonstration that the kingdom of Satan was overthrown. By his coming, the kingdom of God was reestablished on this earth.

Jesus even gives an illustration: the only way to rob a strong man is to first bind him, making him impotent and unable to stop you, and then you can clean him out. Jesus is saying, "When I heal the sick and cast out demons, this is proof to you that Satan (the 'strong man') is bound, and that I am delivering all who have been held captive by him." This means your conversion is proof of the kingship of Jesus. As the church expands across the globe over the centuries, reaching every tongue, tribe, and nation, Jesus continues plundering the "strong man's house." The belief that Jesus has the power to deliver us from hell, but not our day-to-day struggles with our flesh, reveals the weakness of our faith.

In his Space Trilogy, C. S. Lewis did a masterful job of creating science fiction within a biblical worldview. The first book, *Out of the Silent Planet*, finds the hero, Ransom, kidnapped and taken to Mars, portrayed as an unfallen world governed by a powerful angelic being. Beautifully echoing 1 Peter 1:12, the angel has a long closeted conversation with Ransom. The angel is anxious to know of the state of the Earth—the "silent planet"—which has been under siege for millennia and cut off from all communications with the other heavenly spheres. Earth's governing angel had chosen rebellion against the Creator, making slaves of its inhabitants. The angel of Mars knew the Creator executed a secret rescue mission, and eagerly longed for news of the counter-rebellion.

Since the fall of man, Earth has been besieged by the forces of evil. Satan is referred to as the ruler of this world (John 12:31; 14:30; 16:11) and the prince of the power of the air (Ephesians 2:2). Paul emphasizes, "For we do not wrestle against flesh and blood, but against the rulers, against the authorities, against the cosmic powers over this present darkness, against the spiritual forces of evil in the heavenly places" (Ephesians 6:12). Likewise, the book of Job recounts Satan's ability to provoke men to wicked, destructive acts and even to marshal the forces of nature to his devastating ends (see Job 1:12–19).

Listen: The gospel is not only about your personal salvation and relationship with Jesus. It is infinitely bigger than that. The heart of the gospel is God's work in Jesus the Christ to reclaim his fallen creation, delivering it from the hand of Satan and rescuing us from our folly and rebellion. Paul describes the gospel this way, "He has delivered us from the domain of darkness and transferred us to the kingdom of his beloved Son, in whom we have redemption, the forgiveness of sins" (Colossians 1:13–14). The gospel is about the establishment of God's kingdom, overthrowing the usurper and placing the true King on the throne. Although this will ultimately be fulfilled on the last day with the creation of the new heavens and earth, the reign of Jesus the Christ has begun.

The corruption of our sexuality is one of Satan's greatest triumphs, trashing a glorious gift of God and enslaving us at the same time. Your King is calling for your allegiance, inviting you to join the battle and bring the downfall of his enemy. Will you enter the fray?

For Reflection:

1. What does it mean to you that Jesus came to establish God's kingdom? How does this change the scenario for our daily life?

2. How does it make you feel to consider that seeking freedom from your sexual sin is a frontal assault on Satan's kingdom?

3. In what ways are you tempted to see the Christian life as about your personal salvation from hell rather than God's huge, cosmic purposes? What would change if you embraced the bigger picture?

DAY 3: KINGDOM OF THE BELOVED SON

What does the Bible have in view when it talks about the kingdom of God? When the prince of this world chose rebellion and led us astray, the entire created order fell under the curse. Suffering, sickness, and death entered the scene. The brokenness goes beyond humanity; all the earth itself is groaning, longing to be set free (see Romans 8:18–23). Jesus' coming to earth was the beginning of the great reversal. I love this scene from Matthew 11:2–6:

> Now when John [the Baptist] heard in prison about the deeds of the
> Christ, he sent word by his disciples and said to him, "Are you the one
> who is to come, or shall we look for another?" And Jesus answered them,
> "Go and tell John what you hear and see: the blind receive their sight
> and the lame walk, lepers are cleansed and the deaf hear, and the dead are
> raised up, and the poor have good news preached to them. And blessed is
> the one who is not offended by me."

What's going on here? John is in prison because he spoke out against the sexual immorality of the Jewish king, a puppet monarch established by Rome. He is disillusioned, perhaps even despairing. John thought Jesus was going to overthrow the corrupt Jewish leaders and cast out the pagan regime. Instead, John's in prison and ultimately will be executed, his head delivered on a silver platter as a thank-you gift to a dancing girl. He seems to be experiencing a crisis of faith. Very possibly, he's thinking, "It's not supposed to be this way. How could it end like this? Maybe Jesus really *isn't* the one . . . "

How does Jesus respond? By healing physical infirmities, bringing justice to the oppressed and raising the dead, Jesus demonstrates before their eyes that he's setting the world right, and then sends John's disciples back to him in prison to report what they've witnessed. Jesus is undoing all the ways that the world has been broken by the curse, even conquering our greatest enemy—death! In a word, the kingdom of God is overturning the effects of the curse. It's as if Jesus is walking through a bleak, black-and-white world, and everything he touches suddenly blazes in glorious Technicolor. He is bringing life and healing to a sick and dying world. He is "the beginning, the firstborn from the dead, that in everything he might be preeminent" (Colossians 1:18).

But the kingdom is not merely focused on overturning the physical brokenness of this fallen world. Its citizens are central to the kingdom of God. Titus 2:14 describes the purpose of Christ's atonement this way: "[Jesus] gave himself for us to redeem us from all lawlessness and to purify for himself a people for his own possession who are zealous for good works."

Consider this: Jesus went to the cross to purify you for himself. Do you hear the poignant emphasis given in this double declaration? He is purifying *us*, for *his* possession. You and I are central to the plan of redemption. All human history is hurtling forward to the wedding feast of the Lamb (see Revelation 19:6–10). It will be the great consummation of this world and the glorious beginning of the world to come, redeemed humanity sitting down to feast with the Bridegroom, the new and final Adam, beginning the eternal marriage arranged by the Father.

Especially in this stage of redemptive history, the extension of the kingdom is twofold. The number of those who believe and confess that Jesus is Lord continues to grow throughout the world, as the Spirit works through the proclamation of his people and their expressions of love and mercy. Also, within each of us who profess faith in Jesus, his kingdom grows, tearing down our idols and destroying old allegiances as he increasingly rules in our hearts. Jesus' kingdom is not only a future existence, but a present reality!

For Reflection:

1. What are some ways you see the world "groaning" personally? culturally? globally?

2. Do you believe that Jesus' death was for you personally? How does it encourage you to know that gathering a people was central to Jesus' plan—or *does* it? Explain.

3. How does the truth that we're a people for Christ's own possession change our approach to God? What hope can we draw from the fact that this is "the kingdom of the Beloved Son"?

DAY 4: THE REIGNING KING

This week's goal has been to make clear that Jesus' mission was not merely to save souls for some otherworldly existence. He came to redeem the entire cosmos, to remake the heavens and earth. He came to overturn the curse, supplanting Satan as prince of the world and rescuing those held captive by him (see Hebrews 2:14–15). We need to understand that his kingdom *has* come. Although it will not be fully complete until Christ's return, there is a present-tense reality to his kingdom. Jesus is not like David in the Old Testament, anointed by God as king but forced to live in exile until the reign of Saul ended. Jesus defeated Satan and is our reigning King, ruling over the universe for the sake of his church (Ephesians 1:22–23).

Hebrews 2:8–9 makes this reality explicit: "Now in putting everything in subjection to him, he left nothing outside his control. At present, we do not yet see everything in subjection to him. But we see him who for a little while was made lower than the angels, namely Jesus, crowned with glory and honor because of the suffering of death, so that by the grace of God he might taste death for everyone."

Everything is subject to Jesus. As Dutch theologian and statesman Abraham Kuyper declared, "There is not a square inch in the whole domain of our human existence over which Christ, who is Sovereign over all, does not cry: 'Mine!'" But our Hebrews passage makes an important distinction: We don't yet *see* everything as subject to him. The cross and resurrection were definitive. The enemy has been utterly conquered. The end is imminent, but we don't see it yet. To us it looks as if there's a whole lot in this world not yet subject to Jesus. But the Bible reassures us: Jesus *is* ruling. He will accomplish all his purposes, in his timing.

As a teenager, I went camping with a group of friends. To say a couple of my buddies were foolhardy is a gracious understatement. They ran off with our plastic cooler, returning later with four snakes—including two copperheads! Another friend recognized the danger of the snakes, and we hiked out of the woods to a small parking area. There, my buddy carefully dumped them out of the cooler and chopped off their heads with an ax. After getting hacked, one of the copperheads had almost a foot of his body still attached. I vividly remember him slithering toward us, mouth opened wide to snap at whatever he could sink his fangs into, his entrails dragging behind through the gravel.

The devil is doomed, just like that snake. His kingdom is overthrown. Jesus has dealt the death blow. He is now the bound strong man, whose house Jesus is pillaging and will eventually burn to the ground before he builds a new one, more glorious than we can imagine. But if this is true, why is the world such a mess? How can there be so much brokenness in our culture and within each of us?

The devil is still allowed to roam on a fairly long chain. The truth of Christ's reign doesn't mean the war is over. The demise of Satan is written in stone. The new heavens and earth are imminent, but there's still a lot of mopping up to do before the King's return. God has purposes for us *now*, before Jesus' glorious return.

For Reflection:

1. What causes you to question the present reign of Jesus? How would you expect the world to be different if this were true? Where have your desires become demands? In other words, when do you find yourself saying, "If Christianity were true then I would/wouldn't . . . "?

2. What does it mean to you that Satan's kingdom is destroyed? How would your struggle with lust change if you believed that Jesus was reigning, and that through the Spirit victory was within your grasp?

3. In what ways are you resistant to let go and live in the freedom offered by Jesus? How do you believe you'll "miss out" if you surrender?

DAY 5: UNITED TO THE KING

Despite the reality that Satan's reign of tyranny is broken and the kingdom of God is already among us, the Christian life is incredibly hard. Satan is still active, tempting and deceiving. Our culture lures us with promises of pleasure and contentment apart from Jesus. Even more significantly, we betray ourselves. Remember Paul's battle against his flesh in Romans 7? We long to follow our King, but often find ourselves incapable.

What is our hope for growing in obedience? How can we change when we are surrounded by enemies—including our own treacherous hearts? Our hope for lasting change is that Jesus has united himself to us. We've already read that the Spirit prays in groanings too deep for words and that Jesus lives forever interceding for us and serving as our advocate before the Father. But his role in our lives is deeper still. He is united to us in the here and now, enabling us to obey. His resurrection power is ours because he is literally present with us through his Spirit.

In his high priestly prayer, Jesus asked the Father that we would be united with them, even as he is one with the Father (see John 17:20–26). At the Last Supper, while teaching his disciples about the Holy Spirit, Jesus promised the Spirit would dwell in them and that he and the Father would come and make their home with them. He knew persecution was coming, and promised that we would not be left as orphans (see John 14:15–31, especially verse 23). He knows the frailty of our hearts, our inability to serve him in our own strength. He promises to carry us every step of our journey home.

It is only through Christ's strength that we grow in holiness and overcome our struggles with sin. Also, we need his Spirit in order to serve as his ambassadors for the kingdom of God. John 15:1–11 gives the most dynamic illustration of this union. Jesus described himself as the true vine. We are branches connected to him. We are able to bear fruit only as we abide in him. Remember the tree model from Week 3? The Bible uses the metaphor of bearing fruit to describe a life rightly lived for the glory of God. Jesus said the only way this happens is when his life flows into us continually—moment by moment. If we fail to abide, ultimately relying on our own strength and power, any fruit we bear is actually artificial. Jesus said the Father will prune the branches that don't abide in him and throw them in the fire. We need to take this warning very seriously!

So is growth in grace our responsibility or God's activity in our lives? The correct biblical answer is *yes*! The Bible balances realities that our puny minds tend to split into either/or. Consider these passages:

> Therefore, my beloved, as you have always obeyed, so now, not only as in my presence but much more in my absence, work out your own salvation with fear and trembling, for it is God who works in you, both to will and to work for his good pleasure. (Philippians 2:12–13)

> Him we proclaim, warning everyone and teaching everyone with all wisdom, that we may present everyone mature in Christ. For this I toil, struggling with all his energy that he powerfully works within me. (Colossians 1:28–29)

Although dealing with very different circumstances—the first addressing personal sanctification, the latter Paul's labors in ministry—these passages clearly demonstrate the reality that both our personal growth and service to God require intense labor on our part that's utterly dependent on God's action. Paul toils and struggles, even as Jesus works in him. We are all commanded to work out our salvation, but ultimately it's God working in us for his good pleasure.

This mystery is our glorious hope. Jesus kept his promise; we are not alone in this life. In fact, it is in these very places—struggles like sexual sin—where he meets us to demonstrate the fullness of his strength. When Paul and his comrades despaired of life because of their persecution, they learned that God showed up in the midst of these struggles. Thus Paul concluded their persecution "was to make us rely not on ourselves but on God who raises the dead" (2 Corinthians 1:9). Later, speaking of personal trials, he recounts Jesus' words to him, "My grace is sufficient for you, for my power is made perfect in weakness." Paul goes on to boast in his weakness because he learned "when I am weak, then I am strong" (see 2 Corinthians 12:7–10).

Does it feel like your struggle with sexual sin is bigger than you can possibly handle on your own? Good—then maybe you're finally desperate enough to lay hold of Jesus as you never have before! We all need to learn Paul's lesson, that Jesus meets us in our places of most desperate need. Only when we are humble and broken do we let go of any false hope in our own abilities.

Many of us experience victory over sin as new Christians. Why? In those early months, we are as dependent on him, and resting in the gospel, as a newborn baby in his mother's arms. But over time, we shift back toward self-reliance. We begin to feel good about the changes in our life. Self-righteousness sets in. Like Peter trying to walk on the water to Jesus, we take our eyes off him and begin to sink back down into the mire of our sin.

We need to return to our first love and to the radical dependence on God we had at the beginning. Only as we abandon hope in ourselves are we open to the resurrection power of the risen Christ. Jesus is still our deliverer from sin and death—his kingdom has come. Our humility before him unleashes the power of the kingdom in our lives. Are you ready to surrender to your King?

For Reflection:

1. What other circumstances in your life have brought you to your knees? How can you apply the lessons learned through those experiences to your struggle with sexual sin?

2. How do we abide in Christ while laboring and toiling? How can you know whether you are producing genuine or artificial fruit?

3. Do you need to return to your first love? In what ways have you returned to self-reliance since first coming to Jesus? Consider this broadly, beyond your struggle with sexual sin.

WEEK 7:
SURRENDERING TO THE KING

KEY CONCEPT: Because of the fall, the bent of our hearts is to live independently of God. We want to be king over our lives, but this goes against the grain of how we're created. We were designed to serve, therefore we'll either serve Christ or become slaves to our desires.

Still, many obey from very broken places. They live in terror of a God who is only a judge or in response to guilt or in hopes of guaranteeing God's blessing. Genuine obedience flows only from truly knowing God and resting in his love. We can trust this King because he is radically different than any other king in the history of the world. Jesus came to us as a servant and understands life in a broken world, having suffered just as we do. Relationship with him is life-giving. Only his infiniteness can satisfy our insatiable desires.

DAY 1: GOTTA SERVE SOMEBODY

The intent of the past couple weeks has been to give a broader perspective on the work of Christ's redemption. In Week 5, we examined that Jesus didn't simply come to die, but to deliver his people from their slavery to sin and death. He is not a weak Savior, but a conquering deliverer. Last week, we looked at the reality that through the cross and resurrection, Jesus established the kingdom of God in the here and now. He is the reigning King. He brings life to his people, freeing us from the power of sin and death. Although we do not yet see everything under his control, Scripture assures us it is. Jesus rules over all for the good of his church. While confronted with all the ways this world continues to groan for redemption, we're called to live by faith and not by sight, clinging to his promises when our eyes can't see his sovereign hand ruling.

Jesus is not merely "my Savior." His coronation as King gives him ultimate authority. Years ago, in some theological circles, there was debate over whether Jesus could be someone's Savior but not their Lord. And yet, it would have been incomprehensible to the New Testament writers to pose such a question. The very essence of the gospel is that Jesus is Lord. Do you remember the conclusion to Peter's great sermon at Pentecost? "Let all the house of Israel therefore know for certain that God has made him both Lord and Christ, this Jesus whom you crucified" (Acts 2:36). When the Jews sought to bring charges against Paul they declared he was "acting against the decrees of Caesar, saying that there is another king, Jesus" (see Acts 17:1–9). Jesus didn't go to the cross so we could "have our cake and eat it too." Jesus is the Christ—the King to whom we owe our total allegiance.

Although we'd like to believe that we're autonomous, the truth is we're not. Acknowledging that humanity always gives allegiance to either the devil or the Lord, one of my favorite theologians, Bob Dylan, concludes: "You're gonna have to serve somebody."[11]

Because God created us to be stewards over the rest of creation, we're designed to serve. Dylan's point is you are always serving another master. Even those who believe they're serving themselves are ultimately in service to the devil. Indeed, many modern Satanists allegedly don't believe in a real, personal devil—they claim that their worship is centered on serving themselves, indulging their pleasures. Their focus is self-worship.

The tragic irony is that this is exactly what Satan wants. He is at war with God, and his goal is the oppression of humanity. This is accomplished by turning our hearts away from God. Although he sometimes uses direct oppression through evil regimes—ancient Rome, the former Soviet Union, or modern radical Islamic states—he is very pleased to enslave us through our own insatiable desires.

You know the experience of enslavement. Our idols always turn on us. You begin certain behaviors, believing you're in control, only to discover you're a slave and can't stop—even when you want to! Autonomy is a lie. We will always be servants. It's the structure of the universe.

For Reflection:

1. Do you believe that "you gotta serve somebody"? How have you experienced this reality?

2. Does it make you feel like less of a man not to be autonomous? What does this reveal about your understanding of what it means to be a man?

3. If you can accept this hard truth, can you imagine what it would be like to serve your King with joy? How would life be different if serving Jesus was a delight and not a burden? Describe times you've experienced this.

DAY 2: WHY DO YOU OBEY?

When we minimize the work of Christ—seeing it as an abstract, future victory rather than a here-and-now reality—we are not embracing the true power offered to us in the gospel. We need to further address this misconception of what it means to live as a Christian. Many believe it doesn't matter how they live because they're "under the blood," as if Jesus' sacrifice is merely a get-out-of-hell-free card. We claim Jesus as Savior without understanding that Jesus is now King of the universe, redeeming this broken world and offering pardon to his enemies. With the Savior-only mindset, I'm free to live as I please without concern for how God says I am to live.

Here's an example: As a new believer, I ran into an old high-school friend in a pizza shop. When he asked me how I was doing, I told him I was following Jesus. His immediate response was, "Oh yeah, I know all about that. I'm saved too!" And then, without missing a beat, he leaned in close and asked with a gleam in his eye, "Hey, you still dropping acid?"

At some point, my friend had gone forward at an altar call or read a tract and prayed the sinner's prayer, but did he truly know Christ? The gospel had no impact on his life. He didn't see Jesus as a King whose authority must be obeyed. For this man, the gospel was nothing more than fire insurance. Jesus was a Savior who existed to serve *him*, not a King to be obeyed.

If Jesus is the King of the universe, we owe him our total allegiance. He must be obeyed, but the reasons why we obey are critically important. Many Christians feel constrained to obey out of a slavish fear of the consequences for disobedience. Obviously the Bible teaches that the fear of the Lord is good. What we're talking about here is something very different—fear of judgment that stems from a misunderstanding of the gospel and the very character of God. A right "fear of God" is a blessing to his people, so Isaiah prophesied of Jesus that "his delight shall be in the fear of the LORD" (11:3). It means living before God in humility, understanding ourselves as creatures owing allegiance to our Creator.

Those with a warped fear of God believe he is keeping a close eye on them, holding a big stick. They long to indulge their desires, believe they're missing out on what is really good and satisfying in life, but begrudgingly obey out of fear. Until that inevitable moment when temptation is just too strong, or they've been good long enough to deserve a short excursion to the world of pleasure. This attitude powerfully exposes our hearts. We don't believe that God is a God of pleasure, or that Jesus truly offers us abundant life. We really believe God is a killjoy, holding out on us and denying us pleasure. We can hardly be blamed if we eventually indulge, just for a little while, right?

This point was powerfully brought home to me by a brother in my group. As I talked about the pain of my first holiday season two months after my wife's sudden death, I articulated that God made clear to me that I needed to face the pain without running to anesthesia. As I talked about the suffering of that time, he asked, "When is it enough?"

Essentially his question was, "When do we know when we've suffered enough and can finally seek comfort on our own?" I answered that I knew it was enough when Jesus had comforted me, and I didn't need to medicate the pain anymore. The question exposed his heart. "God is not going to satisfy me. He calls me to suffer, but if I really want comfort, I need to find it for myself."

Some of us obey after we fall because we know we're guilty. There was blatant rebellion and now it's time to make up for it. We let God down and need to work hard to get back in his good graces. Even if their formal theology acknowledges the cross of Christ and claims to rest in him alone, their functional theology looks more like penance. There's little joy in the hope of God's forgiveness in Christ; the focus is on personal performance. Nor is there a sense of God's pleasure in their obedience, because it's against the backdrop of their sin and failure. Even in the midst of obedience, the allegiance of their hearts still lies with their sin.

Still others obey because they think they understand the system. They've got God figured out. Like Job's friends, they believe he's all about blessings for obedience and curses for rebellion. As long as they toe the line and conform to God's rules, they can expect the good life. This theology has permeated the American church, leading to extreme forms like the health-and-wealth gospel, but perhaps even more pervasively in subtler varieties encouraging you to expect "your best life now." There is no understanding of the role of suffering in the life of a believer or of the reality that the call of the gospel is an invitation to carry a cross. An even more sinister effect is that it's an attempt to make God my debtor, to manipulate him into doing what I want, like a little boy who obediently helps straighten up because he knows a clean room will be rewarded with a candy bar.

In all these examples of false obedience, our pride is at the forefront. When we see God as a killjoy, we believe we know what will really satisfy our souls. In our response to guilt, there's a trusting in our abilities that flies in the face of the gospel of grace. Our pride is most evident when we think we can play God and manipulate him to get what we want. As you consider the following questions, realize that although you may favor one form of false obedience more than another, most of us tend to bounce between them.

For Reflection:

1. How is your relationship with God characterized by slavish fear, seeing him as an angry judge, ready to slam down the gavel in condemnation?

2. What does obligatory obedience reveal about your view of God? In what ways does this reveal that your relationship with God is focused on personal effort?

3. Are you guilty of toeing the line in order to receive blessing from God? How do you respond when life doesn't go the way you think it should, despite your obedience? What do you think of the idea that you're trying to make God your debtor?

DAY 3: LOVE SO AMAZING, SO DIVINE . . .

In stark contrast to the "obedience" we explored yesterday, the Bible's calling is radically different. First Corinthians 6:12–20 warns against sexual sin, concluding, "You are not your own, for you were bought with a price. So glorify God in your body" (1 Corinthians 6:19–20). But this is not the slavish fear of consequence or obligatory obedience.

Listen to the way 2 Corinthians 5:14–15 describes the Christian life: "For the love of Christ controls us, because we have concluded this: that one has died for all, therefore all have died; and he died for all, that those who live might no longer live for themselves but for him who for their sake died and was raised." Obedience flows not from fear of judgment or obligation, but because we experience the infinite love of God in Jesus. Being bought with a price is not intended to make us feel guilty because of Jesus' sacrifice, but to overwhelm us with his care for us, causing us to rejoice in the love he demonstrated. Through this love of God, we find what we've been desperately seeking in sexual sin. He demonstrates a depth of love, acceptance, delight, and joy in us that we long to receive.

It has been said that the cross shows us two truths simultaneously. When we see the infinite length to which God needed to go to redeem us, we realize we're far worse than we ever imagined. The cross is a bloody mess for a reason. But in the same moment, because the Father was willing to offer up his Son and Jesus endured the cross for the joy set before him, Jesus' sacrifice shows that we are more loved, cherished and delighted in than we would have ever dared to hope. Understanding the gospel means holding both of these truths together simultaneously.

Since my wife's death, the simple gospel message of John 3:16 has meant more to me than ever before. In my loss, I have experienced heartache. Although this term is thrown around all the time, I learned it is an actual feeling. I've experienced a physical pain in my chest that I can't make go away. Unlike the physical experience of nausea that you can relieve by vomiting, this pain persists no matter how much you scream and wail. You can't get it out. In a microscopic way, I am experiencing God's heartbrokenness over this fallen world. Now the sacrifice of Jesus makes sense as never before. In my finiteness, I can't make the pain of my heartache stop. But he is God. At infinite personal cost, the Father, Son, and Spirit conspired together to redeem humanity, reconcile the brokenness, heal the heartache. They could make it stop, and in amazing, sacrificial love, they did.

Jesus told us the Father is looking for people to worship him in spirit and truth (John 4:23–24). He is not looking for slavish, begrudging obedience. He seeks worshippers who, with a deepening understanding of their sin and rebellion, rejoice more fully in the gospel—the goodness and love of God in showing mercy to sinners, taking the initiative to reconcile us through redemption, and establishing his Son as King over all. In love, God paid the price for our redemption, essentially buying us back to free us from the bondage to sin and death in the kingdom of darkness. As we'll examine in detail in Week 11, it's the controlling power and love of Christ that enables and empowers us to change.

Paul provides a powerful contrast between the world and Christians in Philippians 3. Describing people in the world he says, "Their end is destruction, their god is their belly, and they glory in their shame, with minds set on earthly things" (Philippians 3:19). The world is focused on temporal, physical pleasures. They are enslaved by their appetites. Their identity is wrapped up in the very things they should be ashamed of, such as their sexual conquests. But Christians are those "who worship by the Spirit of God and glory in Christ Jesus and put no confidence in the flesh" (Philippians 3:3).

What an amazing definition of what it means to be a Christian! Rather than focusing on our flesh, and being ruled by our appetites, we are called to turn away, placing no hope and confidence in it. Instead of a desperate attempt to prove we're okay and in control, we admit that we're broken individuals. We don't look for joy in our flesh or seek glory through sex because our eyes are opened wide to the glory of God revealed in the face of Jesus Christ (see 2 Corinthians 4:6). His Spirit is at work in our hearts, bringing contentment and leading us to right worship, in spirit and truth. This is the fountain from which genuine, God-honoring obedience flows.

It is only after reveling in who Jesus is and what he accomplished for us that we are then called to respond. We respond in love and joy, realizing that we are "those who live." We have received an invitation to abundant life. Our past was characterized by living for self, in the endless indulgence of our sexual appetite. We have proven to ourselves time and again that there is nothing but dissatisfaction, desolation and despair down this road.

Jesus reveals a radically different path to travel—living not for self, but for him and others. This is the road to freedom. We are created to serve. The Christian life is to bow before our deliverer, this conquering and reigning King, saying, "Command me!" This is why the great hymn "When I Survey the Wondrous Cross" concludes:

> Were the whole realm of nature mine,
> that were a present far too small;
> Love so amazing, so divine
> demands my soul, my life, my all.

True obedience flows from the blessings we receive in Christ and the glorious promises he offers. Ultimately, we obey because we learn that his "steadfast love is better than life" (Psalm 63:3). In him we have found something deeper and sweeter than fleeting physical pleasures.

For Reflection:

1. Review your answers to yesterday's reflection section. How could a focus on the love of God in Christ change your approach to obedience?

2. How hard is it for you to believe that Jesus delights in you? How does it encourage you to consider that you were redeemed in love—that Jesus' love for you is like the delight and anticipation of a bridegroom (see Isaiah 62:3–5)?

3. What would change if your life were focused on worshipping by the Spirit of God, glorying in Christ Jesus and putting no confidence in the flesh? How does understanding Jesus' love make that more attractive?

DAY 4: A RADICALLY DIFFERENT KING

Liberty and self-rule are built into our DNA as American Christians. Our most important national holiday commemorates the signing of the Declaration of Independence, the day we threw down the gauntlet and cast off the tyranny of the English king. Throughout the history of the world, there is a long sordid list of kings who demonstrate why democracy is preferable to monarchy in the modern world. Too often, the royal few horrifically exploit the masses. They live in luxury while the populace lives in squalor. They eat caviar and filet mignon while peasants beg for bread. As Jesus said, "Those who are considered rulers of the Gentiles lord it over them" (Mark 10:42). But then he went on to describe his own wildly countercultural monarchy—greatness in his kingdom means being a servant; those who would be first must be slaves of all. Jesus established this pattern, as he "came not to be served but to serve, and to give his life as a ransom for many" (Mark 10:45).

The glorious thing about our King is that he is radically different than any other monarch in the history of the world. Most monarchs are born into royalty and nurtured in posh palaces. Our King was born in a stable and raised in poverty by peasant parents. He was likely shamed throughout his life with ugly rumors surrounding his premarital conception. Most royalty live with a huge chasm between their life experience and that of every other person under their rule. They have been incredibly fortunate in their birth and have no interest in trading places with anyone else in their kingdom. Here particularly, Jesus is a king like no other. Philippians 2:5–11 describes him as willingly setting aside his glory, not seeing his divinity as something he should cling to. Instead he entered humanity, became a servant and, in a supreme act of humble, loving submission, went to the cross. He chose to identify with God's people by entering into their suffering, experiencing the pain of life under the curse rather than rule from afar.

In the 18th century, American colonists rebelled against England's oppressive "taxation without representation." In stark contrast to the English monarchy, Jesus entered into our experience, being "made like his brothers in every respect" (Hebrews 2:17). He endured suffering, learning obedience and being made perfect by it (Hebrews 2:10; 5:7–10).

We are called to serve a King who poignantly understands our experience. He knows what it's like to walk this earth and suffer under the curse. In Week 5 we looked at how he suffered under temptation, enduring the same temptations that we face, but without ever failing. Because this is true, he knows exactly what we need to endure every temptation we face. This is why we are always promised a way out. Jesus is not absent as you struggle against your flesh. By his Spirit, he is gloriously present to meet you in your temptations, knowing from his own experience exactly the grace you need to overcome them.

But it goes even deeper. We need to take seriously the teaching that Jesus suffered when he was tempted. What does that mean? Many men casually dismiss Jesus' temptation because he was God. They reason that since he was God he was never going to fail, so how hard could it have been for him? Hebrews makes clear: It was hard. None of us have sweat drops of blood, agonizing over the call to obey (see Luke 22:44).

Those who dismiss the depth of Jesus' suffering because of his divinity are misunderstanding what theologians refer to as his two natures. Orthodox Christianity has always maintained that Jesus was both fully human and completely divine at the same moment (and still is, though in a glorified body). We need to fully embrace the reality of both natures of Jesus. It's true— he was God. He was not going to fail. At no point was redemption hanging in the balance despite Satan's desperate attempts. But because he was fully human his temptations were utterly real, and the pull of his flesh was as real for him as it is for you. Just because obedience was guaranteed didn't mean it was easy.

This is a crucial distinction that we need to learn for ourselves in our own walks with Jesus. Because of the cross and resurrection, we're able to honor God in obedience, but we need to let go of the expectation that it's ever easy. Obedience meant suffering for Jesus, and therefore it means suffering for us. When 1 Corinthians 10:13 promises a "way of escape," it is so we will "be able to endure it." In other words, we will still need to fight through it, but we can have the victory. They'll be more on this in Week 11.

For Reflection:

1. In what ways is it hard for you to believe that Jesus suffered the exact same temptations you face? How would your struggle with temptation be different if you believed it?

2. Do you think obedience was easier for Jesus, that his temptations were less severe because he's God? How does this view undermine the reality that Jesus was also fully human?

3. How does the suffering of Jesus—the reality that he willingly put aside his glory to enter our suffering—impact your ability to trust him with your own trials?

DAY 5: GENUINE OBEDIENCE

As we conclude this week, it's my hope that your eyes have been opened more widely to the reality of what Jesus accomplished for us, even here and now, and that you're developing a sense of wonder about who Jesus truly is for us as our King and Redeemer.

The remainder of this book focuses on practical how-to's necessary to restore sexual sanity. But there's a reason we spent so much time focusing on the theological foundation. Genuine obedience only flows when we know that Jesus is the only one worth living for. We obey with joyful abandon only when our greatest joy and pleasure is satisfying him. Until we believe that he is good and committed to blessing us—even through the painful trials of this life— we'll never find joy in obedience, but will always look back over our shoulder at the forbidden pleasures of the world.

Consider how the following passages describe God's goodness toward you, and his ongoing desire to bless you:

> Oh, taste and see that the LORD is good!
>> Blessed is the man who takes refuge in him!
> Oh, fear the LORD, you his saints,
>> for those who fear him have no lack!
> The young lions suffer want and hunger;
>> but those who seek the LORD lack no good thing.
>>
>> (Psalm 34:8–10)

> Trust in the LORD, and do good;
>> dwell in the land and befriend faithfulness.
> Delight yourself in the LORD,
>> and he will give you the desires of your heart. (Psalm 37:3–4)

> How precious is your steadfast love, O God!
>> The children of mankind take refuge in the shadow of your wings.
> They feast on the abundance of your house,
>> and you give them drink from the river of your delights.
> For with you is the fountain of life;
>> in your light do we see light. (Psalm 36:7–9)

You make known to me the path of life;
  in your presence there is fullness of joy;
  at your right hand are pleasures forevermore. (Psalm 16:11)

Admittedly, our experience of life in a fallen world challenges these truths. When we face painful situations and disappointments, in our flesh, we are ready to rail against these claims of God's goodness. But the cross of Jesus Christ won't let us escape so easily. Our God is not the detached Allah of Islam, infinitely removed from the suffering of his people. Our God entered into our suffering, experiencing the pain of the curse and the horror of the divine judgment we deserve in order to redeem us. He loves us and promises to bless us.

Your idols won't die for you. They aren't even alive! Idolaters are mocked throughout the Psalms and Prophets because the people lay prostrate and cry out before hunks of stone that can't see or hear. In Jesus, our Creator was incarnated, taking on flesh and blood, made like his brothers in every way, suffering the pain of death for everyone, so that we can experience eternal life.

He is glorious beyond our capacity to comprehend. Despite our amazing ability to conceive a better universe—one characterized by pleasure, beauty, harmony, fulfillment, with no sin, death, pain, sorrow, injustice—God says you can't even begin to fathom the incredible reality of the world to come (see 1 Corinthians 2:9)! God isn't calling us to live apart from joy and delight, but to find our pleasure and fulfillment in him. We have to give up the finiteness of ourselves—the pathetically fleeting desires of our flesh—but we are offered his infiniteness and pleasures in return. As C. S. Lewis wrote, "Aim at Heaven and you will get Earth 'thrown in': aim at Earth and you will get neither."[12] Those who walk this road begin to partake more and more of both the fullness of this life and the wonder of the life to come.

As we close this week, consider Paul's testimony. Having recounted everything that made him a "rock star" in the conservative Jewish community of the first century, he cast it aside, declaring:

Indeed, I count everything as loss because of the surpassing worth of knowing Christ Jesus my Lord. For his sake I have suffered the loss of all things and count them as rubbish, in order that I may gain Christ and

be found in him, not having a righteousness of my own that comes from
the law, but that which comes through faith in Christ, the righteousness
from God that depends on faith—that I may know him and the power
of his resurrection, and may share his sufferings, becoming like him in
his death, that by any means possible I may attain the resurrection from
the dead. (Philippians 3:8–11)

Do you hear what he's saying? Nothing compares to a relationship with
Jesus. Paul was willing to sacrifice everything because he had found something
so glorious it was even worth dying for! That's why Jesus described the kingdom
as a "pearl of great price" and a "hidden treasure" that was worth selling
everything we own in order to purchase it. This is where joyful obedience
comes from. We were created to revel in his ultimate, infinite beauty and glory.
Think about it: Any object of your lust only mirrors in ridiculously puny ways
the glory of our Creator. We lust because we catch a glimpse of God's beauty
in his creation, and then settle for worshipping that dim reflection instead of
the real thing.

Our infinite God has filled us with desires that seem insatiable only because
we focus them on the finite pleasures of this world. As Samuel Rutherford
wrote:

We seek to thaw our frozen hearts at the cold smoke of the short-timed
creature, and our souls gather neither heat, nor life, nor light; for these
cannot give to us what they have not in themselves. Oh that we could
thrust in through these thorns, and this throng of bastard lovers, and be
ravished and sick of love for Christ![13]

Only God possesses life in himself. Our desires aren't insatiable—they
are infinite. He intends them to be focused on *him*. Only his infiniteness will
satisfy the depth of our desires. Only an infinite love will ultimately bring
contentment to your soul. Hear his promise from Psalm 107:9, "For he
satisfies the longing soul, and the hungry soul he fills with good things." Will
you surrender to this King who in love entered your suffering, walked through
the pain of your trials, offers you the grace to know his joy in the midst of
this life, and in the world to come offers beauty and pleasure that infinitely
transcend your imagination?

For Reflection:

1. What does it mean to you that God invites you to drink from his river of delights? Be honest, and specific.

2. Why is it hard for us to imagine that God is a God of pleasure? What might this reveal about our false beliefs about him?

3. What does it mean to you that any object of your lust is merely a poor reflection of the infinitely greater glory and beauty of its Creator? If this is true, how can you turn temptation into experiences of worship?

SECTION 3:
A NEW BROTHERHOOD

WEEK 8:
WELCOME TO BROTHERHOOD

KEY CONCEPT: The entertainment world bombards us with images of men single-handedly facing cosmic catastrophes with panache. While the rest of us struggle with the reality of our weaknesses, these icons suggest that life's challenges are easily handled alone. However, the Bible teaches that the Christian life should never be lived in isolation. It anticipates that our lives will be radically interconnected, like body parts. Our repeated failure to overcome sexual sin isn't a demonstration of God's inability to deliver, but of our unwillingness to live according to his plan. Furthermore, we live in the midst of a cosmic spiritual battle and need brothers to watch our backs. We're often blind to the depth of the spiritual battle raging around us, as we're seduced by our worldly culture and the desires of our hearts, ever pulling us away from God.

DAY 1: RETHINKING THE MANLY MAN

Why do I like action movies? Because I want to be "that guy"—the one who singlehandedly faces impossible odds, kills his enemies, saves humankind, and rides off into the sunset with the beautiful woman. Much of life feels impossible and overwhelming to me, but that guy is handling situations far worse—with style. Although I'd be dead before the end of the trailer, 007 uncovers the sinister plot, shoots his way through the lackeys, takes out the evil mastermind, and casually orders a martini (shaken, not stirred) when it's all over. The message? Real men can handle whatever life throws at them—on their own. And, as a bonus, they get to have sex with multiple partners without the annoying hindrance of relationships!

Culture challenges us to be the Marlboro Man—riding the range alone, getting the job done, ready to protect the herd from any danger. We're programmed to think that we should be able to face life alone, that we shouldn't need other people. Sometimes we believe we're weak just for feeling like life is hard. Since we were young we've been taught that we should be independent and undaunted by the challenges of life.

To make things worse, we're also told to disengage from our feelings. After all, "Big boys don't cry." When I was six or seven, I remember hearing those words after getting physically hurt. Fighting back the tears, I resolved in my heart that nobody would see me cry again. We receive these messages both directly and indirectly, but we get the point: I should be able to handle life on my own. It's what men do. Life shouldn't hurt. And if it does, there's something wrong with me.

But the hard reality is we are weak, finite creatures. We know our limits (even when we won't admit to them), and often feel stretched to the max. There are many things in life that are overwhelming, and all the unknowns can be terrifying. If we're honest with ourselves, we know we're scared. But rather than admitting this, we posture and pretend we have it altogether. Everyone else is playing the game and we join in, usually assuming that we're the only ones who are acting. But hiding our fears and posturing just makes things worse, adding layers of shame.

I don't know if these messages have deepened in intensity over the years. At least the Lone Ranger had Tonto. But James Bond, Jason Bourne, every Arnold Schwarzenegger character, and most superheroes work alone. They tackle global catastrophes without assistance. But real life doesn't work that way, and it was never *intended* to work that way. At creation, God declared everything to be very good—except for the fact that Adam was alone (see Genesis 2:18). He needed a helper.

Now, this is not saying everyone should marry. Jesus taught that some men would choose singleness for the sake of the kingdom and Paul encouraged believers to stay single for the same reason (Matthew 19:12; 1 Corinthians 7:32–35). God's design goes further than propagating the species or satisfying sexual desire. We are created to live all of life in radical interdependence on one another under him. It is an aspect of what it means to be created in his image—the Trinitarian God who has existed in three persons for all eternity. Over the next couple weeks, we'll examine why God made the church central to the Christian life.

For Reflection:

1. What messages have you heard that reinforce the idea that men should be self-sufficient? How do you try to handle life on your own?

2. When is the last time you asked for help in dealing with a significant problem (spiritual issues, family relationships, work, etc.)? What happened, as a result?

3. How does a self-sufficient outlook impact your interactions with others? How might it prevent you from being honest about your struggles with sexual sin?

DAY 2: RETHINKING CHURCH

For many of us, church is what we do on Sunday morning. "Real life" is disconnected from our "spiritual time," that's squeezed into 10–12 on Sunday. The balance of life is yours—to be lived as you see fit. This may be a tiny step above the idea of the Christian faith as "fire insurance," but beyond the obligation to attend worship on Sunday and certain special church events throughout the year, many see little daily relevance to belonging to the body of Christ.

But perhaps you have greater involvement. You attend a weekly home Bible study or serve on various committees. Maybe you're a leader in the church, responsible for teaching and preaching. While some of us approach church stiff-armed, keeping everyone at a distance, others develop a façade. They wear their game faces anytime they're around fellow members, using service as a fig leaf to hide who they really are on the inside. (We'll look more closely at this next week.)

But God's plan is for the church to live in radical interdependence. Consider this example from the early church: "And they devoted themselves to the apostles' teaching and the fellowship, to the breaking of bread and the prayers. . . . And day by day, attending the temple together and breaking bread in their homes, they received their food with glad and generous hearts" (Acts 2:42, 46). And listen to Paul's description of his ministry among the Thessalonians: "So, being affectionately desirous of you, we were ready to share with you not only the gospel of God but also our own selves, because you had become very dear to us." He describes himself as a "nursing mother" and "a father with his children" (1 Thessalonians 2:7, 8, 11). When Paul ministered to believers, his life was bound with theirs. It wasn't restricted to a few hours on certain days of the week.

Here's the point: our faith isn't only personal. Jesus didn't die for isolated individuals—he died for the church. Consider the metaphors used throughout the New Testament. God's people are one body, with Christ as the Head (1 Corinthians 12:27). We are living stones being built into a spiritual house (1 Peter 2:5). We are a chosen race, a royal priesthood, a holy nation, a people for his own possession, so that we may proclaim the excellencies of him who called us out of darkness into his marvelous light (1 Peter 2:9).

The vast majority of New Testament metaphors focus not on the personal, but rather corporate dimension of our faith. However, it's unlike any other "corporation." It doesn't mean that all Christians work for the same company while remaining in isolated cubicles, focused on individual projects. God's design is far more dynamic. We're to be radically interconnected and dependent on one another.

Paul could not have used a more powerful metaphor than the human body. First Corinthians 12:12–26 gives a poignant description of what it means to be a part of the church. Paul begins by observing that the body is made up of many parts that are incredibly varied in their purpose, function, and even usefulness. But he goes on to show how each part needs the others. The eye can't say to the hand, "I don't need you." Even those that seem to be weaker are indispensable. If you've ever smashed the tip of your finger and lost the nail, you know how necessary this seemingly insignificant part of the body truly is.

Ephesians 4:15–16 also uses the body metaphor to describe our spiritual growth as a community event. Often we think that reaching spiritual maturity is our own responsibility. Scripture teaches that we need the involvement of the entire body in order to become spiritually mature. Growth happens only when each part is working properly. Spiritual development requires the whole body of Christ.

It's amazing how Scripture holds together the intricacy of our faith in ways that often don't make sense to us on the surface. For example, we may ask, "Is growth as a Christian my personal responsibility, or is it the responsibility of the entire body?" The correct biblical answer is "Yes!" Consider Colossians 2:19. Paul is speaking against the spiritual arrogance of members of the church who are pleased with their morality, or rather, self-made religion. He says they are "not holding fast to the Head, from whom the whole body, nourished and knit together through its joints and ligaments, grows with a growth that is from God." The Bible describes a radical interdependence on one another, as God works in us and through our relationships to bring us to maturity. We need each other! We'll look at this more closely next week, but this reality highlights the importance of finding a church that takes discipleship and community life very seriously.

For Reflection:

1. In what ways are you tempted to view the Christian life as a "me and Jesus" affair? How is that attitude encouraged in the church? How is it challenged?

2. Do you believe that you need the body of Christ to reach maturity? In what ways have you experienced this reality?

3. How would your life change if you embraced your need for the body of Christ? How would this impact your priorities, your use of time, etc.?

DAY 3: ANYONE HERE BEEN IN THE ARMY?

We've looked at the reality that as men, we're culturally programmed to be loners—at least when it comes to asking for help. In contrast, the Bible says the Christian life is radically interdependent. Why? Although we'll consider a number of issues over the next two weeks, a crucial starting point is that we are living in a world at war. In Week 5, we saw that Satan is referred to as the ruler of this world. The Bible tells us that the usurper has been cast down and that Jesus is now pillaging the strong man's house. But consider these passages written to us, who live after the establishment of Christ's kingdom, but awaiting his final return:

> "But woe to you, O earth and sea, for the devil has come down
> to you in great wrath, because he knows that his time is short!"
> (Revelation 12:12b)

> Be sober-minded; be watchful. Your adversary the devil prowls
> around like a roaring lion, seeking someone to devour. Resist him,
> firm in your faith, knowing that the same kinds of suffering are
> being experienced by your brotherhood throughout the world. (1
> Peter 5:8–9)

> Finally, be strong in the Lord and in the strength of his might. Put on
> the whole armor of God, that you may be able to stand against the
> schemes of the devil. For we do not wrestle against flesh and blood, but
> against the rulers, against the authorities, against the cosmic powers
> over this present darkness, against the spiritual forces of evil in the
> heavenly places. Therefore take up the whole armor of God, that you
> may be able to withstand in the evil day, and having done all, to stand
> firm. (Ephesians 6:10–13)

We live in a cosmos at war. We need each other because life in this world is not a warm, fuzzy existence. We're in a battle and we're taking fire. We live in the middle of a spiritual barrage, so we need brothers to watch our backs.

There is a powerful scene in the film *Gladiator*. General Maximus and his fellow gladiators arrive in Rome and go to fight in the famous Collosseum. The announcer proclaims to the crowds that there will be a reenactment of Rome's victory over Carthage, introducing Maximus and company as the "barbarian hoard"—in other words, not the side you want to be on! Maximus quickly sizes up the situation, asking, "Anyone here been in the army?" He wants to know if anyone knows how to fight as a unit, declaring, "Whatever comes out of these gates, we've got a better chance of survival if we work together. Do you understand? If we stay together we survive." They do fight together and "rewrite" history, defeating the Roman charioteers.

Peter compares the devil to a roaring lion on the prowl. Do you know who lions attack? They pounce on the weak and sickly, the young, anyone straggling behind the rest of the pack. We are called to spur one another on (see Hebrews 10:24 NIV). We need each other in this battle. Alone, we will end up straggling behind and falling prey to our ravenous foe. If we stay together, we survive.

This is not to detract from the reality that Jesus is our deliverer and reigning King. Our current era of redemptive history can be compared to the events at the close of World War II. When the Allies stormed the beaches in Normandy on D-Day (June 6, 1944), retaking France, they effectively broke the back of the Nazis' stronghold in Europe. With that great victory, the outcome of the war was certain. But V-E Day didn't happen until the following May. It took almost another year to drive the Nazis back into Germany and capture Berlin.

Spiritually, this is where we are in redemptive history. The ruler of this world is conquered. Jesus triumphed over the principalities and powers of darkness, making a mockery of them. You don't need to fear "for he who is in you is greater than he who is in the world" (1 John 4:4). But there is still resistance. Our enemy will not stop fighting until they are utterly vanquished, banished to the pit forever. Just as the Nazis continued fighting until the battle was at the doorstep of their own capital city, so our enemy will continue to fight—filled with wrath and malice toward God and his people—until Jesus destroys him forever.

But it goes even further. We have a glorious role in extending the kingdom of Christ and vanquishing evil from the world. I love this promise from Romans 16:20, "The God of peace will soon crush Satan under your feet." It is the work of God to crush our enemy, but he is using *us* in the operation—and indeed, will crush Satan under *our* feet! What a glorious hope and promise!

For Reflection:

1. How would your life change if you were more mindful of this truth—that the devil is filled with rage because his time is short, and that he's literally hell-bent on destroying you and those you love? How would a deeper awareness of this reality impact your day-to-day priorities?

2. Do your relationships with other men in the church demonstrate this reality? Are there men battling alongside you, or do your relationships look more like a peace-time barbecue? How would your relationships need to change in order to reflect life in a cosmos at war?

3. What's your reaction to the promise of Romans 16:20? How can this hope impact your battle against temptation? How would it feel to have Satan's head under your heel, instead of his claws around your throat?

DAY 4: NO COMMANDOS IN THIS ARMY

Most of us don't begin battling sexual sin by seeking help. In fact, we might spend decades unsuccessfully trying to conquer these issues on our own. There are a number of reasons we do this. Part of it stems from our desire to tackle life single-handedly, coupled with the cultural messages we looked at earlier this week. Also, we have so much shame surrounding our sexual sin; we believe we're alone in this struggle and that no one else will truly understand. None of us want to be exposed at our worst, so we cover our shame, presenting a façade of spiritual health and joy, living a lie before others. But what's the result? Because change happens in the context of community, we stay stuck in our sin. We need other people in our lives in order to grow.

I suspect you've struggled with feelings of despair over your sin. You've tried reading the Bible, praying, memorizing Scripture, fasting, all to no avail. Even if you experience short-term victory, eventually you find yourself pursuing those same old sins. Why is long-term change so elusive? Because you're not seeking to change the way God calls you to—through fellowship with the body of Christ.

This in no way diminishes the power of the gospel. Often we believe that because God is all-powerful, we should be able to just pray and *zap*—he'll eradicate the sin from our lives. We even promise to publicly testify and give him all the glory once we're delivered. But that isn't God's design. Thus, as we remain stuck in sin, we begin to question his power and goodness. We doubt our own salvation because our struggle with sin persists, even though the Bible describes us as dead to sin. How do we reckon with this reality?

The problem is not that God's power is limited, or that he is somehow indifferent to our plight in suffering with sin. Nor does it follow that because you struggle, you're not in Christ. In fact, experiencing a sense of guilt and longing for change is often a demonstration of the Spirit's presence. Prior to coming to faith, I was pretty content and remorseless in my sexual sin.

Here's the thing: By going it alone, you're not pursuing change the way God prescribes. Antibiotics are wonderful tools to help us overcome sickness, but we need to follow the prescription carefully: Take them at the appropriate intervals and take them all—don't stop halfway just because you start feeling better! God's power is unlimited, but we still need to follow his design. He is, after all, God. It works his way, not ours. It's not that God is unable to change us, he's just unwilling to do it according to our design. His ultimate goal is to deal with the even deeper issues of our hearts.

Consider this challenge from Proverbs 18:1, "Whoever isolates himself seeks his own desire; he breaks out against all sound judgment." Do you hear that? When we isolate ourselves in our sin, choosing to keep it hidden from others, we're seeking our own desire. It means we're choosing to stay stuck.

So, what desire are we really seeking? If we're honest, our pride keeps us silent. We're more concerned about our reputation and how others perceive us. Maintaining our façade is more important than pursuing genuine change for the glory of Jesus. Our pride is the deeper issue that matters most to God. One of the reasons he's determined that change must happen in the context of community is so we'll humble ourselves and acknowledge our struggle with sin to one another (more on this in Week 14).

Of course, our isolation might also expose a subversive desire to hold on to our sexual sin. When we're isolated in our sin, we have no one to answer to, no one asking us hard questions, no one monitoring what we do online. Our isolation leaves the door wide open to run back to our sin whenever we like, while we half-heartedly pursue change. This is why the proverb concludes that isolating ourselves is insanity! Community is the only road to sexual sanity.

We'll discuss this in more detail, but for now realize that if you're truly going to do battle with your sin, it can't be in isolation. According to Scripture, the first step of personal change is to be intentional about pursuing real relationships in the body of Christ. If you're unwilling to do this, then you had better acknowledge that you're not truly serious about overcoming your struggle with sin.

For Reflection:

1. How have you isolated yourself from others in your sin? What façades do you present to others—good husband, father, ministry leader, etc.?

2. What positive examples have you seen in the church of people receiving spiritual care to help them overcome struggles with sin? What would make you feel safe to disclose your own struggles?

3. How is pride at work in your isolation? Are you willing to sacrifice your good reputation to overcome your struggle with sin? What does your attitude reveal about your heart and the depth of your faith?

DAY 5: ENTERING THE FRAY

Given the relative peace and prosperity of American culture, it's hard for us to get our minds around the idea of living in a cosmos at war. I spoke with a brother from India who said that compared to life in his country, American Christians are "living heaven on earth." It's different for us.

However, Christians in the Muslim world and elsewhere who are facing persecution are quite mindful of the reality of spiritual warfare. In a very real sense, they're facing the beast of Revelation. Regardless of your views on the end times, I suspect all Christians agree with John that "many antichrists have come" (1 John 2:18), some wielding the oppressive, political power attributed to the beast. But there is another, subtler kind of spiritual warfare.

In the book *Worldliness: Resisting the Seduction of a Fallen World*, Dave Harvey tells of an African brother who came from extreme poverty and persecution to study in America. How do you think he responded to his newfound freedom and prosperity? He said it is harder to be a faithful Christian in America than in Africa![14] I attended seminary with a brother from China who'd been imprisoned multiple times for preaching Christ. He was asked to contrast his experience in China with life in America. He said, "In America, you just have a different kind of chains."

We need to see this: While we must continue praying for and assisting our brothers and sisters facing persecution every day around the world at the hands of the beast, we must never lose sight that we too are being continually, strategically seduced:

> And he carried me away in the Spirit into a wilderness, and I saw a woman sitting on a scarlet beast that was full of blasphemous names, and it had seven heads and ten horns. The woman was arrayed in purple and scarlet, and adorned with gold and jewels and pearls, holding in her hand a golden cup full of abominations and the impurities of her sexual immorality. And on her forehead was written a name of mystery: "Babylon the great, mother of prostitutes and of earth's abominations." And I saw the woman, drunk with the blood of the saints, the blood of the martyrs of Jesus. (Revelation 17:3–6a)

In our culture, we are free from political persecution, but the warfare is still intense. We are confronted with the whore who seduces us with entertainment, materialism, sexuality, food, drink, and ease. Her goal is to distract and enslave. Flipping the calling of Colossians 3:1–2 on its head, her mission is to take our focus off seeking "the things that are above, where Christ is." She wants us to set our minds on things that are below, not on things that are in heaven. If we're not bound for hell, she at least wants us impotent for the kingdom while on earth!

Of course in all of this, our flesh is active. The secular, unbelieving world is putty in Satan's hands, but our own sinful hearts become engaged and lead us astray. Temptation's lure is effective because our hearts are ever ready to turn from the worship of the one true God for an idol. How is the whore alluring you? Sexual sin is just one way. Our hearts are naturally wired to live for self, and our spiritual foe knows our bent and is at work daily to exploit our weakness. There are so many ways we seek to medicate the pain of life in a fallen world—food, entertainment, sports, work, home-improvement projects. I heard of one marriage that fell apart because the husband compulsively bought Christian books! Our nature is to take any number of good things and turn them into idols. They may even be wonderful things intended to take us deeper into worship of God, but when they are divorced from him and become ends in themselves, they are deeply broken and destructive. For example, when my colleague and dear brother, Bob Heywood, began dealing with his pornography addiction (as an elder in his church), God also convicted him that he had made an idol out of theology! He had begun to study Scripture and God in a way that was removed from a growing relationship with him.

Over the next couple weeks, we'll further examine why life in the church is God's divine plan for our growth to spiritual maturity. But first you need to embrace this truth: You have an enemy who is literally hell-bent on your destruction. Are you going into battle alone? If we stay together, we survive.

For Reflection:

1. In what areas of life besides sex are you most at risk of being led astray—sports/entertainment, stuff, success, food, money, hobbies? What keeps your eyes focused on earth instead of heaven?

2. What good things in your life are you tempted to turn into idols—ministry, biblical/theological study, relationships, work?

3. What tangible steps can you take to combat the ways you're seduced by the world? Who can you recruit to join the battle? Ask God to show you two or three men who can be intentional about fighting alongside you.

WEEK 9:
REDEMPTIVE COMMUNITY

KEY CONCEPT: So many in the church hide behind a façade, pretending to have it all together. We even buy into the lie we project to others, minimizing our sexual sin and believing it really isn't a big deal. We forget that Jesus welcomed the sexually broken and reserved his most scathing indictments for the religious hypocrites.

Although many Christian testimonies give the appearance that everything was a mess before Jesus and now they live in victory, God doesn't wave a wand over any of us at conversion. The Christian life means having an increasing awareness of our need for his grace to live differently—and a growing humility that makes us willing to listen to others and have our sin exposed. Only when we're secure in God's love and mercy toward us will we face the worst about ourselves.

DAY 1: WORSHIP IN A COUNTRY CLUB

The intent of Section 3 is to examine the importance of the body of Christ in seeking freedom from sexual sin. Last week, we examined the stark biblical truth that we are not living in a peacetime reality. We're in the middle of a war that's cosmic in scope, making World War II insignificant by comparison. This week, we examine our need for others not just to cover our backs and help us stand against our spiritual foe, but to help us fight the enemy within.

This is why it's so important for the culture of your church to fit with your desire to live in sexual purity. Too many churches function like country clubs. You attend church with others of your same age, race, and especially social class. Everyone dresses up and maintains an air of reserved cordiality. It's a place for the beautiful, "together" people who have life all figured out.

Everyone looks nice, smells nice, and respects appropriate social decorum. And these same façades apply even if you go to church wearing jeans and a T-shirt.

If you ask unbelievers to describe Christians or the church, they'll invariably talk about our moral stance on cultural issues (and our corresponding hypocrisy—more on that below). All too often the message our culture hears from the church is "Come in here and be good like us." Too many of us go to church every week pretending everything is fine, hiding our sinful habits behind nice clothes and fake smiles. We look like we're heading out for brunch at the country club. We prefer hiding behind a façade to letting others know who we truly are.

The crazy underside of this is: Everyone in these churches is wrestling with sin in secret. No one's honest about what's really going on. While they hide behind the illusion of a perfect family, successful career, and pristinely manicured property, they're slowly dying inside because they know they're a bunch of frauds. A further tragic irony of this state of affairs is that even as you know you're living like a hypocrite, you nevertheless grow more proud of your outward behavior—which makes honesty even more difficult.

John describes this as "walk[ing] in darkness" (1 John 1:6). We deceive ourselves and lie to others. Not only do we hide the truth of who we are, but we actually begin to believe the lie—all the while becoming more proud of the façade we've constructed to hide our shame and deceive others. And the more elaborate the façade, the grimmer the contrast with who we truly are, and the less likely that we'll come clean and let people know the truth of our struggles. The result is a relentless cycle of hypocrisy, deceit, and despair, spinning out of control.

We need to take this posturing very seriously. Reading through the Gospels, we see Jesus showing love to all the social outcasts. Whether leper or prostitute, Jesus responded to all with love and tenderness. He never rejected anyone who pleaded for mercy. Everyone who came to Christ for help received it. What's the one notable exception? He railed against the self-righteous hypocrisy of the religious establishment! He was utterly unimpressed with all their formal religious behaviors. Matthew 23 recounts Jesus preaching a scathing sermon against the religious leaders—the scribes and Pharisees. He described them as "whitewashed tombs, which outwardly appear beautiful, but within are full of dead people's bones and all uncleanness" (Matthew 23:27). Perhaps most pointed for those of us struggling with sexual sin in the church, he challenged them, "For you clean the outside of the cup and the plate, but inside they are full of greed and self-indulgence" (Matthew 23:25). What is our lust if not greed for things not ours to possess, and our behavior a graphic example of self-indulgence?

As we discussed in earlier weeks, our sexuality is a demonstration of our spiritual allegiance. But this truth goes even deeper. The scariest place in the universe is to posture in the church as righteous, when in truth our lives are filled with sin. We'll discuss John's call to walk in the light in detail in Week 12, but for now suffice it to say we need to be ruthlessly honest about our struggle with sin. Our honesty is a demonstration of the genuineness of our faith in Christ. Jesus declared, "The light has come into the world, and people loved the darkness rather than the light because their deeds were evil" (John 3:19). Are you hiding your sin in the dark, or bringing it into the light?

For Reflection:

1. In what ways are you deceived by your own façade—minimizing your sexual sin and focusing instead on all the "good" things about you?

2. Do you believe that your sexual behavior reveals the spiritual allegiance of your heart? Explain your answer.

3. Does Jesus' challenge to the Pharisees in Matthew 23 scare you? How does your life demonstrate hypocrisy? How are your private and public personas different?

4. Are there behaviors in your life that you are continuing to hide—even from this group? If so, what would make you willing to bring them into the light?

DAY 2: WORSHIP IN A HOSPITAL

In stark contrast to the country clubs we often find, churches should be more like hospitals. What do you find in hospitals? People groaning, writhing in pain, bleeding, and soiling their clothes. Proper decorum is out the window because people are dying. The focus is saving lives. People in a hospital are expected to be a mess. In fact, only the (literally) insane enter insisting they're fine. This is not to say that a hospital is the *only* contemporary metaphor—making disciples means a lot more than this. Nonetheless, it's crucial to understand that all Christians continue to struggle with indwelling sin, and need others to help them grow in holiness.

Jesus does not wave a wand over anyone when they come to faith. The brand-new Christian getting up from his knees after the altar call still has all the same struggles with sin that he had on his way down the aisle. This is not to deny the reality that Jesus often removes huge chains from our lives at our conversion. By God's grace, the night I came to faith I walked away from over a decade-long struggle with substance abuse and never looked back. We love a good testimony of radical transformation, but here's the thing: After I came to faith, I needed brothers and sisters in Christ to teach me how to live. The Technicolor sins in my life like drugs and sexual promiscuity were just the tip of the iceberg.

There's a subtle expectation in many churches that once people are in Christ, they should have their lives together and significant struggles with sin should be in their past. As a consequence, too many Christians begin their walks with Christ in humble dependence, but quickly return to self-effort. We need to hear Paul's warning to the Galatians, "Let me ask you only this: Did you receive the Spirit by works of the law or by hearing with faith? Are you so foolish? Having begun by the Spirit, are you now being perfected by the flesh?" (Galatians 3:2–3). As we examined last week, our desire for independence runs deep. We resist depending on others—including God. It is a profound picture of the depravity of our hearts that as God begins to bring change, we grow proud, exalt ourselves over our pagan culture (and weaker brothers and sisters in Christ), start applauding how good we've become, and continue on our merry way, trusting our own strength apart from humble reliance on his continued grace.

Christians need the gospel. The hope of God's grace in Christ is not just what gets us into heaven; it is the power through which we are called to live the Christian life. "Therefore, as you received Christ Jesus the Lord, so walk in him, rooted and built up in him and established in the faith, just as you were taught, abounding in thanksgiving" (Colossians 2:6–7). Do you hear what Paul's saying? We're supposed to live out the Christian life in the same way we started—receiving through faith the grace and mercy of God through Christ. Surrendering to the lordship of Christ is the foundation of our faith, and our lifelong calling is to continue walking in the Spirit with a simple, childlike trust in his power, goodness and mercy. Our churches need to continue preaching the gospel to Christians, not offering the gospel to unbelievers and then calling the saints to live by the law in their own strength.

So many men live under condemnation because of their struggle with sin. They think they know what they should look like as Christian men. They're weighed down not only by the sins they commit, but all the things they think they should do. Here's what *Jesus* said we should do: "This is the work of God, that you believe in him whom he has sent" (John 6:29). The "work" that God calls us to do is first and foremost to believe in Jesus, to rest in the promise that in him "we have redemption, the forgiveness of sins" (Colossians 1:14). We're called to live out of the great promise of Romans 5:1, "Therefore, since we have been justified by faith, we have peace with God through our Lord Jesus Christ." True obedience in the Christian life flows only from this gospel fountain. Until we rest in what Jesus has done in reconciling us to God, we'll slavishly obey out of fear, all the while growing more bitter that we're forbidden to indulge in the sin we crave.

Further, when the Bible talks about the grace of God, it does not have in view only mercy. Too many Christians have flattened grace to mean "God forgives my sin." But God's grace is infinitely bigger. It is the power offered to us to live differently in this life—which is why even Jesus, though sinless, is described as having the grace of God resting on him (Luke 2:40 NIV). We begin the Christian life desperately dependent on the mercy of God's grace, and we're called to continue walking in desperate dependence on his gracious power to sustain and transform us. I've worked with so many men who complain that God demands the impossible. Change *is* impossible for us, but we were never intended to live on our own strength. We desperately need his power—and one another.

What I'm about to say, I don't say lightly: Too many Christians spend their lives church-hopping—looking for just the right music, the most eloquent or dynamic preacher, the most exciting kids' program. We shouldn't approach church as consumers (more on this next week). *But*, if you're not in a church that brings you weekly to the feet of Christ for mercy and healing and hope, you might want to prayerfully consider finding another church. Likewise, if you can't be totally candid with your pastor about your sexual sin, you may need to find another church.

One important disclaimer: You won't know whether your church, or any other, is a "safe place" until you muster the courage and risk *sharing* your struggle with someone. If you're considering leaving your church, I challenge you to first open up to your pastor. At the very least, it will expose how much your own shame and pride might be masquerading as "spiritual discernment." Before you bail, show your pastor the consideration of opening your heart to him. You might be pleasantly surprised.

For Reflection:

1. Does your church focus on behavioral change and following the rules, or does it focus on lifting up Jesus as our only hope? How do you think your pastor would describe the process of life change?

2. Do you remember a time when your response to your sin was to praise God for his great mercy in Christ? What prevents you now from overflowing with gratitude in the face of your sin?

3. Do you view God's grace only as mercy? How would it change your perspective to realize that Jesus knows just what you need in temptation and offers you real power for the battle?

DAY 3: REDEMPTIVE COMMUNITY

As we began to examine last week, the Christian life is designed to be a community effort. Section 1 of this book looked at how the world is suffering under the curse, eagerly awaiting the great work of cosmic renewal promised at the end of time (see Romans 8:19–23). Looking to that glorious end, the church is called to be a redemptive community, building on the foundation of Christ and his apostles by overturning the effects of the curse in the world. We're invited to take part in the great work of extending the kingdom of God. This of course includes evangelism and intentional discipleship, but it is so much more than a focus on "spiritual" things. Extending the kingdom includes tangible ways that Christians should be tending creation as God's stewards, the great calling to care for the poor, not to mention all the exciting ways we're invited to transform our culture by using our gifts for God's glory. All of these are crucial to growing out of our sin and into Christ. There is much to be done.

The extension of the kingdom has two aspects—it is both spreading the gospel and kingdom blessings in the world, and having God's kingdom expand in our own lives. God's ultimate goal is to conform each of us into the image of Christ. Romans 8:28 gives a wonderful promise: "And we know that for those who love God all things work together for good, for those who are called according to his purpose."

Christians love to quote this verse (and put it on coffee mugs, usually surrounded by a heart-shaped wreath of flowers). But here's the problem: Typically, we're focused on *our* definition of good, not God's. Think about it. When you say you've had a good day, what do you mean? You didn't get stuck in traffic; your boss wasn't a jerk; you got the project done that'd been hanging over you. A good day is when everything falls into place and goes your way, right?

Here's the problem: God's definition is radically different. And it comes in the much less frequently quoted next verse: "For those whom he foreknew he also predestined to be conformed to the image of his Son, in order that he might be the firstborn among many brothers." God's definition of good is to radically transform his people, making them like Christ, so Jesus will be surrounded by brothers and sisters for all eternity. *That's* what God means by good.

Being conformed to the image of Christ corresponds with the two great commandments to love God and others, both of which require us to be in relationships in the body of Christ. We become men who are holy, set apart for

God, putting off sin and putting on righteousness, living our lives to his glory. Likewise, we become people who are focused on blessing others rather than serving self. We'll focus on the latter piece next week. The next two days will focus on our need for the body of Christ to help us change personally.

For Reflection:

1. What's your reaction to the idea that the calling of the church is to spread the kingdom of Christ and overturn the effects of the curse? How can you be active in tangible ways to extend Christ's kingdom in your family, workplace, neighborhood, etc.?

2. How do you define "good"? How do you respond to God and others when your kind of "good" doesn't happen?

3. What areas in your life would you personally label "not good"? How would life be different if you believed Romans 8:28–29 and allowed these circumstances and relationships to conform you to the image of Jesus? In what ways are God's purposes radically counter to your own?

DAY 4: WE NEED A MIRROR

One of the tragic ironies of sin is how we're often blind to the ways it's at work in our own lives. This is particularly true with our relations to one another. One of my colleagues at Harvest USA is from Ireland. A while ago she posted a helpful Irish proverb in our break area: "A friend's eye is a good mirror."

We need other people's input to see ourselves rightly. All of us know the experience of being around an obnoxious person who's absolutely oblivious to his behavior. You've been to parties where someone kept trying to hold the spotlight, blind to their self-centeredness—and everyone else's boredom. But in reality, we all live with *huge* blind spots. It's like we all have spiritual bad breath. There are things about us that reek, but unless someone else addresses the situation, we live in ignorance. We need brothers and sisters in our lives who will give us the spiritual equivalent of a breath mint and let us know when things are so bad that we need to get to the dentist.

There is a wild, but true, fundamental reality to our existence: In significant ways, other people know us better than we know ourselves—your spouse, children, extended family, even coworkers and neighbors. You are completely blind to areas of sin in your life that they see plainly. Don't be deceived that because you're successfully hiding certain behaviors, therefore you're so much smarter than everyone else and have them fooled. Others see sin that you can't see, and although they may not be aware of all your behaviors, they know something's very wrong.

My most hated "Christian" T-shirt is the one with a drop of blood spattered across the chest with the words, "Just one drop of Jesus' blood washed away my sin!" Jesus didn't prick his little finger and shake off a single drop of blood to redeem you. He needed to be taken outside the city, stripped naked, lifted up on the cross, and slaughtered—for *you*. That is the harsh truth.

The late Jack Miller, pastor and professor at Westminster Seminary, was famous for saying, "Cheer up! You're much worse than you think!" This is the central truth of our humanity. We are so desperately broken and lost in sin that nothing short of the death of the Son of God suffices to pay for our sin. I know you *know* this, but does this truth make a difference in how you actually *live*?

All this to say, we shouldn't be surprised how blind we are to our sin. We come to faith in the first place because God in his mercy opened our eyes to the reality of our sin and enabled us to perceive that Jesus atoned for it at the cross. In other words, we've been blind all along. But then, we forget how broken we are and become comfortable. Perhaps God rooted out some big sin areas in your life soon after conversion—substance abuse, sexual activity, lying, stealing, cursing, getting in fights—but sin goes far deeper than outward behavior. Sadly, as God cleans up our outward lives, we often grow self-assured and proud of how "good" we've become. This can become a downward spiral.

As our outward behavior improves two things can happen: 1) Sin often goes underground and begins to pop up only in the secret places of your life. Sexual sin is a great example. Thus, we tend to work even harder at all the outward, public demonstrations of "righteousness"—a fig leaf covering the shame of our secret life. 2) Even if our behavioral sin has dramatically improved, our relational sin often goes unaddressed. We ignore the challenges of our wife and others to see how loveless and self-centered we are, because we're content with our record of good deeds. The tendency of married men to neglect their primary calling to their wives and children and instead throwing themselves into their careers, or the work of the church (especially those in full-time ministry), makes Isaiah's scathing indictment that "all our righteous acts are like filthy rags" (Isaiah 64:6 NIV) particularly pointed. And the better we feel about our outward façade, the less willing we become to honestly receive criticism for our sin.

Although most Christians acknowledge that indwelling sin is an ongoing problem, we tend to deny, justify, or make excuses when someone points out *our* specific sin issue or pattern. We're ready to acknowledge the presence of sin in the abstract, but we reject direct challenges. Again, our struggle with sexual sin is a great example. We inwardly justify our behavior with innumerable excuses—it's not that big a deal, we're not hurting anyone, etc. We're quick to minimize the problem or blame our spouse. We desperately need others to help us see the severity of our behavior, with this sin and all the others we're totally blind to.

For Reflection:

1. Do you believe that others know you better than you know yourself? Who are those specific individuals? Are you listening to them? Why or why not?

2. Can you remember a time when someone challenged you on a sin you were previously unaware of? How did you respond? Why?

3. Outside of sexual sin, what patterns of behavior have friends and family challenged you about? Do they have a point, or do you think they're off-base? Explain.

DAY 5: FACING OUR BLINDNESS

In his teaching against judging others, Jesus makes the reality of our spiritual blindness explicit:

> Why do you see the speck that is in your brother's eye, but do not notice the log that is in your own eye? Or how can you say to your brother, "Let me take the speck out of your eye," when there is the log in your own eye? You hypocrite, first take the log out of your own eye, and then you will see clearly to take the speck out of your brother's eye. (Matthew 7:3–5)

Notice that Jesus never denies the man's uncanny ability to accurately spot a speck in somebody else's eye (even though he has a log in his own). The parable cuts both ways. It points to our utter blindness to our own sin and yet, paradoxically, shows that we're often able to rightly discern sin in others. The exhortation is to ruthlessly stamp out *our* sin, even as we work to help others root out theirs.

The only way for you to effectively remove the log from your eye is to be willing to face the worst things about yourself without shrinking back or making excuses. Have you noticed, at least in others, how desperate we are to avoid this? How many celebrities have you seen publicly declare that they have no regrets and wouldn't change a thing? How many politicians steadfastly defend their own honor in the face of blatant lies and exposure? Is there anyone with the courage to face the log in his eye? We can only do this when we rest in the gospel, trusting in the finished work of Christ. Apart from him, we trust in our own record. We're convinced that it's up to us to measure up. We refuse to admit failures because they impugn the record and reputation we're so desperate to establish. And anyone who tries to challenge us on sin is a threat.

Jesus put it this way, "And this is the judgment: the light has come into the world, and people loved the darkness rather than the light because their deeds were evil. For everyone who does wicked things hates the light and does not come to the light, lest his deeds should be exposed" (John 3:19–20). When our hope is in our performance, we prefer the darkness of ignorance. We keep our sin hidden, fighting tooth and nail against others who dare to challenge the false front we've constructed.

Most Christians understand this reality theologically, but the only way this truth gets any traction in your life is if you're willing to listen to others. It is one thing to give intellectual assent to doctrine, quite another to apply truth to our lives. How do you respond when you're challenged about sin in your life? Your response demonstrates the extent to which the gospel has sunk into your heart. Apart from applying and practicing doctrine, it is meaningless. You may acknowledge a belief in total depravity, the reality of your spiritual blindness, and the ongoing sin in the life of a believer, but your unwillingness to heed the challenges of others reveals the truth you carry in your heart.

The gospel radically subverts that dynamic. The cross of Christ is the most damning indictment against our reputation imaginable. Jesus suffered hell for us because the righteousness of God demanded that someone must pay for sin.

To again paraphrase Jack Miller: The cross of Christ is a bloody mess, showing us that we're far worse than we would have ever imagined, so bad that the Son of God needed to be slaughtered for our redemption. But at the same time it gloriously reveals that we are more loved, cherished and delighted in than we would have ever dared hope, because Jesus willingly—for the joy set before him—went to the cross to redeem us. Embracing that simple truth enables us to face the worst things about ourselves because on one hand we know that our sin was atoned for. And on the other hand, as we trust in the peace and reconciliation we have with God, we are free from the slavery of our own record and reputation. We have the love and approval of the only One who ultimately matters. We have a surety in the finished work of Christ that gives us the courage to face the log in our own eye and get out the ax.

So, we will always need brothers and sisters in Christ to help us see the things we can't see. Our personal faith and confidence in Christ enables us to live openly in relationship with others, receiving the criticism and challenge to the indwelling sin in our life that we so desperately need in order to be conformed to his image. Do you see how all of this hangs together?

For Reflection:

1. How do you tend to respond when someone challenges you on sin—isolate, get defensive, make excuses, get angry, something else? What does your response reveal about how the gospel needs to sink deeper into your heart?

2. What prevents you from trusting the work of Christ? How does the disapproval of others (past or present) impact your ability to believe God's love for you?

3. What would your life be like if you were free from worrying about your reputation? Free from the fear of others' disapproval? Free to own your failures honestly instead of making excuses for them?

WEEK 10:
SERVANT SOLDIERS

KEY CONCEPT: Our culture encourages a "me-first" attitude that runs completely counter to God's calling upon our lives. In stark contrast, God calls us to follow Jesus and to lay down our lives to serve others for his glory. Although some of us serve God for broken reasons—as penance for our failings, or to hide our sexual sin behind a façade of good works—it's undeniable that God calls us to serve others for his sake. As we learn to sacrifice our own agenda of serving self and to put others first, God changes our hearts. We need to cultivate a servant's heart in all our relationships, because just as indulging our flesh leaves us desolate, serving others roots out our sin and opens the door to the fullness and joy that we've always longed for in this life because it draws us closer in relationship with him.

DAY 1: THE CHURCH: HAVE IT YOUR WAY?

"Have it your way." "You deserve a break today." The promises made to us by advertisers are endless, pandering to our desires, seducing us into believing that their product is the key to the happiness that eluded us—until now. Advertising often fans the flames of our idolatry on two levels: First, it tempts us to believe that a created thing can satisfy our souls, subverting true worship of our Creator (see Paul's definition of idolatry in Romans 1:18–25). Second, advertising encourages us to continue putting self at the center. This is already the bane of humanity's existence, and it is particularly aggravated in those of us who struggle with sexual sin.

Advertising feeds our idolatry and innate selfishness, impacting life in 21st century Western culture in profound ways—not least of all, how we approach the church. We're tempted to approach church as consumers. Do we like the preacher's style and delivery? Does the music conform to what we believe the Bible proscribes or stimulate the experience we want to have in Sunday worship? Is there a lively singles ministry? Is the youth group exciting for teens? Does children's Sunday school make the Bible fun? These and dozens of other questions inform our decisions when we are looking for a church.

Choosing a church is one of the most crucial life decisions we make. Therefore, important factors need to be considered. Your church should believe the Bible is God's Word. The preacher should proclaim Christ and him crucified. As discussed last week, the gospel should be held forth as the only hope for living as a Christian. There should be an emphasis on building community and the importance of living as a Christian within the body of Christ. You should be encouraged by God's love for you and desire to be known by you, and be challenged to build deeper intimacy with him. In other words, the primary focus in the decision-making process should be Christ and his kingdom, and our role in it—not whether the church scratches our particular itch for teaching, music, or programs. God doesn't call us to a church to devour a spiritual product, but to enter into deep, intimate, serving relationships with one another for the extension of his kingdom in us as a community (our sanctification) and to extend the kingdom to an unbelieving world by proclaiming the hope of reconciliation to God the Father through Jesus Christ, and tangibly through deeds of love and mercy (evangelism).

The most memorable moment in John F. Kennedy's inaugural address was his concluding challenge, "And so, my fellow Americans, ask not what your country can do for you—ask what you can do for your country."[15] Similarly, we should not look for a church that exists only to serve our needs, asking only what it can do for us. We should be eagerly looking for that place where we can use our gifts to glorify God and bless our brothers and sisters in Christ.

For Reflection:

1. What do you look for in a church? How might this reflect a consumer mindset?

2. What spiritual gifts has God given you? How are you currently using your gifts in your local church?

3. Can you recount a time when you felt used by God with the gifts he's given you? Explain.

DAY 2: BEFORE YOU SERVE . . .

The remainder of this week will focus on one of the redemptive ways we grow out of our struggle with sexual sin—by responding to God's call to serve him in the body of Christ. But before we get there, we need to briefly address one of the persistent problems with our service in the body—serving out of guilt and shame.

When we feel particularly guilty about our sin, many of us throw ourselves into serving Christ as a means of penance. Perhaps you volunteer for a particularly dreaded ministry responsibility (like teaching the three- and four-year-olds in Sunday school) or spend Saturday afternoons handing out gospel tracts in the local mall after acting out the night before. We're trying to prove our love for God and demonstrate sorrow over our sin. But this response flies in the face of the gospel! In effect, rather than resting on the work of Christ, you're trying to atone for your sin through good works. You're trying to reestablish your record as a good guy, instead of embracing the harsh reality evidenced by your sin and guilt. We are decidedly *not* good guys, because even in Christ there are vestiges of our old selves. On some level, we're still men who delight in sin. But praise God that he sent a deliverer to free us from this body of death.

Other times we use ministry as a fig leaf. It becomes the thing that covers our shame. We struggle with the reality of who we are in private with our secret sins, so we engage in ministry activity to create an illusion. Yesterday we discussed how church folk often show a façade to one another on Sunday morning. What we're talking about here is more involved than wearing a fake smile to worship. It is doing ministry publicly to hide who we are privately.

This is the exact opposite of how Jesus taught us to live. In the Sermon on the Mount (see Matthew 6:1–18), Jesus begins his discussion of religious activity by warning that if we act piously for men to see, we will not receive a reward from our Father in heaven. As he lays out our calling to give to the poor, pray and fast, he concludes with the command that these things be done in secret stating, "And your Father who sees in secret will reward you." This passage is a sober warning. First, it bluntly describes the truth we know intuitively but try to avoid: We live our lives before the face of God whether we like it or not. He is the God who sees in secret. We can't even hide our thoughts from him. He knows not only everything we do, but everything we'd like to do and wish we'd done. The motives of our heart are exposed before him. Therefore, he calls us to serve him secretly because he knows how two-faced we are. He knows that much of who we are publicly is tainted by mixed motives.

Where does this issue come to roost specifically for men like us struggling with sexual sin? So many men who come to see me describe themselves as good Christian husbands, fathers, and leaders in the church, with just this "one little problem" back in the dark corner of their soul. According to Jesus, that dark, little secret says more about who we truly are than any other aspect of our lives. This passage should sober any of us who think that our outward ministry is more important than our inner thoughts and secret behavior. Jesus makes it clear that our private behaviors reveal who we truly are, and that God will reward us accordingly. Further, our commitment to hide that truth behind the fig leaf of Christian service stands as an additional indictment against us.

How do you know when ministry is a fig leaf or a heartfelt response to the gospel? We'll discuss this at length in Week 11, but consider these questions: Is your life characterized by compartmentalization? Are you hiding certain behaviors so that you're one person in private and someone radically different in public? Are there things in your life that you hide from others on your ministry team? If you're answering yes to these questions, that's a pretty good indicator that you're hiding behind fig leaves.

Huge, seemingly successful ministries have been built out of guilt and shame, hiding the truth of a secret struggle, only to come crumbling down in the face of exposure. First Corinthians 3:10–15 makes clear that on the last day all ministry will be tested—and revealed to be of lasting eternal value, or only the temporal illusion of worth destroyed in judgment. This is not to say that there isn't a genuine faith and desire to serve God in the midst of it all, but there is also pride and an unwillingness to be truly known. Ministry should be the fruit of our relationship with Christ, flowing from the fullness we have in him. Fig-leaf ministry is brutally destructive to our souls because, rather than flowing from our relationship with Jesus, it's used to hide the absence of real vitality in that relationship—all the while pretending before others that it exists. We become hypocrites in the darkest, most destructive sense. There is nothing more dangerous than teaching the Word and not obeying it!

Why we do something is as important to God as what we do. In fact, it can be argued that our motivation is even more important. Remember the time Jesus observed people giving in the temple? As the rich put their gifts into the offering box, he saw a poor widow put in two small copper coins, and said, "Truly, I tell you, this poor widow has put in more than all of them. For they all contributed out of their abundance, but she out of her poverty put in all she had to live on" (Luke 21:3–4). From a worldly vantage point her gift was ridiculously miniscule, but it was infinitely more valuable to God than all the extravagant gifts of the wealthy.

In John 4:23–24, Jesus said our Father is looking for people who will worship him in spirit and truth. In all our worship and ministry, what is going on in our hearts matters more than our behavior. In tragic irony, the harder you work in the face of your sin, the more separated you become from your hope for deliverance. Only by coming to Jesus with open, blood-stained hands—again and again and again—softens our heart to his mercy. Only his grace ultimately delivers us.

Consider this passage from Titus 2:11–12: "For the grace of God has appeared, bringing salvation for all people, training us to renounce ungodliness and worldly passions, and to live self-controlled, upright and godly lives in the present age." Do you hear what Paul is saying? Only through understanding the grace of God are we enabled to overcome our struggle with sin. As we discussed in Week 9, Day 2, his grace is the divine power we need to be victorious in our battle with sin.

Until we get our hearts around this reality and learn to rest in the gospel, we'll continue doing penance and stitching fig leaves. Only knowing the love of God and resting in his grace effectively deals with our guilt and shame, freeing us from this relentless cycle.

For Reflection:

1. When have you found yourself doing more ministry out of a sense of guilt? What's it like to be engaged in ministry when you're feeling guilty?

2. Where have you used ministry as a fig leaf? Who are the brothers who honestly know the depth of your struggles? How would it feel to tell those you serve alongside that you're doing this study?

3. How would you define God's grace? How does the Titus 2 passage speak to you? How does life change happen?

DAY 3: DYING TO SERVE

We need the body of Christ in order to grow. But there are two sides to this reality. Last week we talked about our own blindness, and our need for brothers to open our eyes to our sin. At the same time, we have a role in sharpening others.

Consider Ephesians 2:8–10: "For by grace you have been saved through faith. And this is not your own doing; it is the gift of God, not a result of works, so that no one may boast. For we are his workmanship, created in Christ Jesus for good works, which God prepared beforehand, that we should walk in them." This passage is frequently quoted to prove that our salvation is a free gift from God—we can't do anything to earn it, so there is no room for boasting. And as such, it's a good reminder to those of us who wear fig leaves and do penance. But do you see where Paul goes with his argument? He tells the Ephesians they've been saved by grace not works, in order that they may begin to *do good works*. We're saved by grace in order to serve God in unique ways that he prepared for us beforehand.

This is an awesome calling and a glorious hope. I'm continually amazed by this truth. Although raised in a Christian home, I was a slave to my sexual sin for many years before coming to faith. All the while, God knew the ministry he had in store for me. He planned beforehand how he would redeem even my rebellion against him, for my good and his glory!

The Titus 2 passage quoted yesterday points to the same conclusion. It begins by making clear that it's God's grace that enables us to turn from sin and live righteously, but watch how it continues:

> For the grace of God has appeared, bringing salvation for all people, training us to renounce ungodliness and worldly passions, and to live self-controlled, upright and godly lives in the present age, waiting for our blessed hope, the appearing of the glory of our great God and Savior Jesus Christ who gave himself for us to redeem us from all lawlessness and to purify for himself a people for his own possession who are zealous for good works. (Titus 2:11–14)

Jesus is looking for a purified people, zealous to serve him, their motives flowing from their relationship with him. A people "possessed" by Jesus, filled with wonder at his redemption and the joyful expectation of his return. Again, our motivation for service is crucial, but service is indispensable. It is a hallmark of the Christian life. If you are in Christ, he's given you gifts to serve his body.

Why does this matter? A significant way we overcome our struggle with sin is by beginning to serve others. Think about it: We've lived consumed by our pursuit of personal pleasure. We've trampled others in the process, even those dearest to us. God calls us to radically subvert this dynamic by becoming men who lay down our lives for others—men who, by his grace and empowered by his Spirit, face the tremendous challenge to learn the joy of living selfless lives. This is an indispensable aspect of growing in spiritual maturity, a way we burn off the fat of our flesh and put on the muscle of the Spirit.

Jesus perfectly demonstrated a life of selfless service. Consider the following contrast from the life of Christ: Immediately after his baptism, Jesus was led by the Spirit into the desert to be tempted by Satan for forty days. He fasted the entire time. In case you don't get the point, Matthew and Luke make it explicit, "And after fasting forty days and forty nights, he was hungry" (Matthew 4:2). You probably know the story. The devil begins by going after his obvious physical weakness, urging him to turn stones into bread. Jesus responds, "Man shall not live by bread alone, but by every word that comes from the mouth of God" (Matthew 4:4). Jesus is literally starving. He certainly had much less body fat to burn than the average American, so his body had probably been feeding off living tissue for days to stay alive. But he still refuses to lift a finger to satisfy his very real need.

Now fast-forward several months. Jesus has begun his formal ministry. Crowds are flocking from everywhere for healing and to hear this One who teaches with authority. On one particular day, a huge crowd followed him to a desolate place, invading his solitude as he mourned the death of his cousin John the Baptist. After listening to him teach all day, they were hungry. They had probably only missed two meals, but what does he do? He miraculously produces a feast of bread and fish, feeding well over the five thousand recorded (women and children were left out of the head count, so the crowd could easily have been triple the size).

Do you see the amazing contrast? When he's literally starving, he doesn't feed himself, but trusts his Father to provide (who eventually does send angels to care for him—a very significant point!). But when he's confronted with a crowd who went a single afternoon without food, what does he do? Bread and fish in abundance. A huge feast with twelve basketfuls left over! This is such a glorious picture of how we are called to live—focused not on our own satisfaction, but on pleasing others.

We examined last week that God's ultimate goal for our life is to conform us to the image of Jesus. What does this mean? He is calling us to be servants and lay down our lives for others. Look at Mark 10:42–45:

> And Jesus called them to him and said to them, "You know that those who are considered rulers of the Gentiles lord it over them, and their great ones exercise authority over them. But it shall not be so among you. But whoever would be great among you must be your servant, and whoever would be first among you must be slave of all. For even the Son of Man came not to be served but to serve, and to give his life as a ransom for many."

Although this passage is usually cited as a proof text that Jesus' sacrificial death was central to his mission, this ignores the context entirely. Jesus is not primarily seeking to prove the atonement here—he's describing what it means to be his follower. Just as Jesus laid down his life for others, those who are his disciples are called to walk in the same way. We follow in his steps when we lay down our lives in the service of others.

For Reflection:

1. How does the call to serve Christ and others change your perspective on the Christian life? How does it subvert the all-too-typical American evangelical approach to church discussed in Day 1?

2. How would focusing your life on serving others impact your struggle with sexual sin? Be specific.

3. Beyond sexual behavior, how would your life change if your focus was on serving others rather than personal pleasure? Consider your closest relationships—family and extended family, close friends, coworkers, neighbors, etc.

DAY 4: PETS ARE A GOOD IDEA

I'm disappointed, because one of my daughters is allergic to any pet but fish. I would like to have a dog. Even a cat would be better than nothing. Why? Besides being fun, caring for an animal helps us remember what it means to be human. As discussed back in Week 3, God has created us to be his image-bearers. He established us to rule over his creation. In a sense, we serve as his representative to the rest of the created order. To subdue the earth doesn't mean to exploit it however we like, but to see that nature and our fellow creatures are properly cared for. Caring for a pet, providing for its needs, and teaching it to obey are distinctly human, yet God-given desires. They help us remember that we serve under another and are called to do God's bidding.

Further, caring for a pet gives us a unique glimpse into the heart of God. Animals require great patience. They are foolish, driven by their impulses and pleasures. They are, after all, dumb animals. But we develop great affection for them. There's a reason that God compares us to sheep and describes himself as the Shepherd—and it's not because we're cute and fuzzy!

A lot has been written on the stupidity of sheep. They seem to have a relentless drive to wander off, while lacking the ability to find their way home. They'll climb to precarious places when they spot some exciting vegetation, but are often incapable of getting back down after their treat, sometimes getting stuck before they even reach the coveted prize. They tear up even the roots of the grass, destroying any future sustenance.

We're foolish in much the same sense. We're ruled by our passions and pleasures. From a sexual standpoint, we chase our desires into places that will kill us. In our insatiableness, we completely squander the good gift of sex. And the only way we get back home is when the Shepherd pursues and rescues us, carrying us back.

Service to God's people goes much deeper in the same direction. Perhaps the sweetest example of this is parenting. We have godlike status to our kids—especially when they're infants. Nothing makes this so poignantly clear than when we hold a tiny baby who's utterly dependent on us in every way. She can't even get out a burp without help! But what do we discover? A love deeper than anything we've known for this tiny person who is literally a part of us. And it's not the shared DNA—close friends who have adopted children describe the same depth of affection for their kids. Our selfless service and sacrificial love enables us to taste the glory and pleasure of God (and his pain as well). As we serve in dependence on him and for his glory, we are increasingly conformed to the glory of Jesus.

This wonder is not restricted to those blessed to become parents. Singles and couples without children are invited to learn the same glorious lesson through loving others, apart from any natural familial connection. All of us are called to serve selflessly in the body of Christ—and the wider world. This is evangelism at its best. God uses our service to help us understand our place in this world as his image-bearers, to open our eyes wider to his glory, and to enable us to begin tasting in deeper ways the wonder of his love in Christ Jesus.

For Reflection:

1. Have you had the experience of raising a pet? What did it teach you about patience, perseverance, and compassion? How did you experience a growing affection for your pet through those actions?

2. Have you ever held a baby and pondered the reality that you were once that helpless and dependent? What would change if you realized that you're as needy and dependent on God, moment by moment, as an infant is on his parents?

3. How has your experience with pets, children—anyone dependent on you—impacted your understanding of God and his love?

DAY 5: SERVING SLAYS SIN

We grow to love those whom we serve. The world would have us believe the exact opposite: If you can find someone you really love, then you will be delighted to serve them. But our selfishness can never be conquered by affection and fuzzy feelings. Often, the reason we fall in love in the first place is that we believe this other person will really satisfy *me* sexually, make *me* happy, make *me* feel complete. In other words, the very starting point is radically self-focused.

We first need to conquer our selfishness, then affection flows—even to the most unexpected places. I remember hearing a pastor describe how his love for his congregation grew as he committed to serve them selflessly. He found himself pursuing leisure time with difficult people from the church on his day off, because he had grown to truly love them and enjoy their company. Being committed to serving Jesus by serving his people changes our hearts toward them and deepens our love for him—and at the same time, begins to diminish our love for ourselves. Learning to serve means learning to love and, as love begins to obliterate our selfishness, it sounds the death knell to sexual sin.

Listen! God is calling you to let go of something you love, but he wants you to see how small and pathetic your idol is compared to his fullness. The devil wants you to believe that you'll be left empty and desolate. What a lie from the pit of hell! You're *already* empty in your sin, and you know it. Life is *already* a desperate search for fulfillment in what feels like a wasteland.

God is showing us the way to abundance. Ironically, it comes through dying to ourselves—letting go of our desires and the sins that we love, in order to serve God and others. It's the very thing we've fought so hard to avoid. Next week, we'll examine the reality that life on God's terms *is* hard. You're not signing up for an easy ride. In some ways it will be harder, but it is still infinitely better.

Consider this promise—what God offers if you're willing to relinquish life on your terms and embrace the reality of life on his terms:

> For this reason I bow my knees before the Father, from whom
> every family in heaven and on earth is named, that according to the

riches of his glory he may grant you to be strengthened with power through his Spirit in your inner being, so that Christ may dwell in your hearts through faith—that you, being rooted and grounded in love, may have strength to comprehend with all the saints what is the breadth and length and height and depth, and to know the love of Christ that surpasses knowledge, that you may be filled with all the fullness of God. (Ephesians 3:14–19)

We'll focus more on this passage next week, particularly the promise that we'll "be strengthened with power through his Spirit." This is crucial, because apart from a deep reliance and growing intimacy with Christ through the Spirit, our service looks like the broken examples discussed earlier this week. Did you catch the kind of life being offered to us in this passage? As Christ dwells in us by faith, we're rooted and grounded in love, God reveals Jesus in deeper ways, opening our eyes to the wonders of the universe, drawing us into the mysteries sought by humanity and never discovered until now. What are the glories of this mystery? Christ in *us*!

God worked in Jesus to reconcile the broken relationships of humanity, both to himself and to one another. He is promising to restore *shalom* to this broken world, and this ultimately means becoming *our* God. He is offering us nothing short of himself! Any created things you've ever desired, even good things, have only been desirable to you because *he* is desirable. Your heart is only delighting because it has caught a miniscule glimpse of the beauty, majesty, strength, and glory of God. He wants to give you your heart's desire. The problem is that we're confused about what will truly bring joy to our souls. Consider the promise: "filled with all the fullness of God." And it will only be found in this relationship with him as we are committed to laying down our lives to serve him and others—obeying the two Great Commandments.

For Reflection:

1. When have you served someone you really couldn't stand? Did it soften your heart or make things worse? Did you find yourself praying more to God for the ability to serve graciously, or grumbling to others? Be specific.

2. How has serving others made you more dependent on God? How has it deepened your relationship with him?

3. Are you encouraged to consider that God offers you himself, or does that seem too abstract? Have you ever experienced joy as you considered who God is, what he did for you in Jesus, and the promises of what awaits you in the life to come? Explain.

SECTION 4:
A TRANSFORMED LIFE

WEEK 11:
ARE YOU READY TO FIGHT?

KEY CONCEPT: Many Christians expect that obedience should be easier. When confronted with behaviors that seem impossible to overcome, we often sit passively on the sidelines, waiting for God to act. However, there's a reason Scripture uses athletic metaphors for the Christian life. Like training for a marathon, growth in grace is hard work. But it's where God meets us, enabling us to do the impossible. The Christian life is a fight. Overcoming sin will always feel like death, but because of the incarnation, Jesus understands this perfectly. He suffered through temptation victoriously. He knows the grace we need to obey. And he gives us his Spirit to empower us, making obedience possible.

DAY 1: TIME TO GET BLOODY

"In your struggle against sin you have not yet resisted to the point of shedding your blood" (Hebrews 12:4).

In his book *Wild at Heart*, John Eldredge makes a good observation: As men we want to be adored as knights, but we don't want to bleed like them.[16] Are you ready for the fight?

So far, we've looked at our descent into slavery to sexual sin (Section 1), the work of our deliverer to free us from bondage (Section 2), and the necessity of our brothers in Christ to help us win the victory (Section 3). This final section is all about *you*. That is, God is calling *you* to give everything you have in the war against sexual sin. This is the most significant battle you're facing right now. Every other significant spiritual fight in your life is hanging on the outcome of this battle. You know it's true. We've looked at the fact that the battle against sin is far subtler and deeper than your sexual behavior, but the reality is, you can't even begin plumbing the depths of your heart while you're mired in the sewer of your sin. You know that as long as you're devouring the rotting, maggoty carcass of your sin, you have no stomach for God's feast. Remember Proverbs 9:13–18? Lady Folly promises a feast, but doesn't tell you that it takes place in a tomb.

Maybe you're exhausted because you feel like you've been fighting without much success. My first question to you is: Are you fighting alone? If so, take another look at Section 3. You can't possibly win this battle alone. You weren't designed to fight as a lone commando. Perhaps you've let people in, but continue to fail. Or maybe you're thinking along the lines of so many other men, "I know I can't do this. God needs to do this, so I'm waiting for him to act." It's as if we can continue in our sin until God finally zaps us and makes it easy to obey. Here's the straight dope: *That is never going to happen.* Growing in obedience and surrendering big sin areas to God will never be easy (at least at first). It will always be painful, always a sacrifice. It will always feel like death.

So I ask again: Are you ready to fight?

The reality is, God has already acted on our behalf. We examined the work of Christ in Section 2. He is our deliverer who conquered Satan and freed us from both death and the power of sin. Again, this doesn't mean obedience is easy. It wasn't easy for Jesus either! But Jesus' victory means that obedience is now possible. Before coming to faith, there was no option but to continue as slaves to sin. Now victory is ours—if we're willing to fight.

In this life, spiritual maturity is an arduous process that requires consistent, strenuous effort. There's a reason Scripture uses athletic metaphors. Listen to the apostle Paul's descriptions of his life in Christ:

> Do you not know that in a race all the runners compete, but only
> one receives the prize? So run that you may obtain it. Every athlete
> exercises self-control in all things. They do it to receive a perishable
> wreath, but we an imperishable. So I do not run aimlessly; I do not
> box as one beating the air. But I discipline my body and keep it under
> control, lest after preaching to others I myself should be disqualified.
> (1 Corinthians 9:24–27)

> Brothers, I do not consider that I have made it my own. But one
> thing I do: forgetting what lies behind and straining forward to what

lies ahead, I press on toward the goal for the prize of the upward call
of God in Christ Jesus. (Philippians 3:13–14)

The Christian life was hard work for Paul. The Greek text for
1 Corinthians 9:27 is particularly poignant. A closer translation would read, "I
pummel my body and make it a slave." Consider the months of daily, hardcore
training necessary to prepare for a marathon. Paul is saying that still only
approximates what is in view with our spiritual conditioning. And the goal of
our striving is so much more glorious! We need to heed Jesus' words about the
severity of our battle with sin—it would be better to gouge out our eyes and
cut off our hands and feet, going to heaven blind and maimed, than to let these
parts lead us into sin so that we go to hell able-bodied (see Matthew 18:7–9).
We are called to a brutal, intense battle against our sin. But God doesn't leave
us alone in the fight.

For Reflection:

1. Do you wish the Christian life were easier? In what ways? How might
this expectation keep you stuck in sin?

2. How does the challenge of obedience affect your relationship with God? Does it make you angry with him? Does it seem like he asks the impossible? Why?

3. What messages do you get from your church about the Christian life? Do you get the idea that obedience is easy and that no one else is struggling with sin like you, or do you hear other Christians talk honestly about their struggles to obey? Explain.

DAY 2: ADJUSTING EXPECTATIONS

I've interacted with a number of men who've made comments along the lines of, "I know I need to put Jesus where porn is in my life," or "I need to desire Jesus instead of desiring other men." From a theological standpoint, there is an element of truth in these statements. They acknowledge that our sexual sin is idolatry, worshipping created things instead of our Creator. Our false worship must be replaced by true worship. As one author wrote, "[T]he young man who rings the bell at the brothel is unconsciously looking for God."[17] Although there's truth in these statements, we need to realize that this is not a simple apples-to-apples parallel.

Although we do need to replace our love of sin with right worship, at the same time you need to realize that Jesus is *not* going to become like porn for you. There are two related reasons why it doesn't work this way. First, the Christian life is always by faith. One of the reasons we go in sinful directions is that God doesn't deliver the way we want. Living in essentially a desert climate, the Israelites probably enjoyed worshipping God in his temple as long as he kept sending rain. It was when the rain stopped that it became attractive to slink off to the "high places" in the hills to have sex with a shrine prostitute in front of the pagan fertility gods. It was something tangible. Something they could *do*. They didn't have to just wait and pray—they could seemingly take steps to make things work.

Now, think of it in a 21st-century context. One man who struggled with sex and substance abuse described rising before the sun and having wonderful fellowship times with God. But then he went out and worked all day in the summer sun. At 5 a.m. he loves communion with God, but at 5 p.m. obedience is hard. After a long hot day in the sun, he's got two options—go home to his shabby little sauna of an apartment to eat a TV dinner alone (with a God he can't see), or go to a dark, air-conditioned bar "where everybody knows his name," have an ice-cold beer in front of him before he even asks for it, and a cute waitress flirting with him as she delivers a hot roast-beef sandwich with steak fries. Which sounds more desirable in the moment? When life is hard, our idols seem to deliver faster.

So here's the problem: Jesus will never become a quick fix for you like sexual sin—that's the reason we become mired in sin decades after coming to faith in Jesus. We must live by faith, believing God ultimately blesses our costly obedience, because in the moment it can be excruciating—it certainly doesn't feel like *life*. This is why Hebrews 11:6 says, "And without faith it is impossible to please him, for whoever would draw near to God must believe that he exists and that he rewards those who seek him." Sitting in the hot, little apartment alone feels like death. We need to realize something: Jesus will never deliver for us the way that sexual sin does. That's why it's not enough to say, "I have to replace porn with Jesus." Jesus will not give you a thrill every time you choose to obey. Morning devotions are not regularly a glorious mountaintop experience. But you will have an orgasm every time you sin. We need to be realistic about the challenge of obedience. This is what Scripture has in view when it repeatedly tells us to wait on God.

So, Jesus will not become porn for you. But at the same time, the Christian life isn't all drudgery with the distant hope that you'll go to heaven when you die. It is glorious! Through obedience, God offers us joy and contentment that infinitely surpasses the fleeting pleasure of sin. This is because we only experience the delight of relationship with him when we are willing to obey. And the joy he gives is pure—bringing peace to our soul, leaving no guilty stain to blot our conscience and poison our relationships after a momentary thrill. Porn, fantasy, and illicit sex are always great in the moment, but what's the end result? Your desires are insatiable. After hours in front of the monitor you're always left wanting more and only the increased guilt, neglected sleep, or pressing responsibilities pull you away. If you've had poison ivy, you know how great it feels to scratch—even better to blast scalding water on it—but it provides only temporary relief that actually enflames the rash further. Sexual sin works the same way. The fleeting pleasure doesn't bring satisfaction; it leaves only greater hunger, now coupled with guilt and shame.

Here's the second reason that we can't just replace sin with Jesus. He *wants* us to go through these hard times. There is value to our suffering through temptation. You're probably familiar with the passage in which Jesus calls us to be ruthless in stamping out sin in our lives, but listen to how he begins:

> Woe to the world for temptations to sin! For it is necessary that
> temptations come, but woe to the one by whom the temptation
> comes! And if your hand or your foot causes you to sin, cut it off
> and throw it away. It is better for you to enter life crippled or lame

than with two hands or two feet to be thrown into the eternal fire.
And if your eye causes you to sin, tear it out and throw it away. It
is better for you to enter life with one eye than with two eyes to be
thrown into the hell of fire. (Matthew 18:7–9)

Did you catch that? Jesus said it is *necessary* that temptations come. We're
being sharpened through these experiences. Our Father is committed to
conforming us to the image of Jesus so for all eternity he will be the firstborn
among many brothers. This is God's will for us and he declares this to be
good. God promises that our suffering through temptation is for our good. It
accomplishes his purposes in our lives—conforming us to the image of Jesus,
building spiritual muscle, preparing us to serve in the body of Christ, and
fitting us for the new heavens and earth.

The 17ᵗʰ century Scottish theologian Samuel Rutherford wrote, "I find it to be
most true, that the greatest temptation out of hell is to live without temptations.
If my waters should stand, they would rot. Faith is the better of the free air, and of
the sharp winter storm in its face. Grace withereth without adversity. The devil is
but God's master fencer, to teach us to handle our weapons."[18] There is no growth
in holiness without a fight. If we long to hear, "Well done, good and faithful
servant," we need to battle the temptations that war against our souls! We will
only arrive in heaven sweaty, caked with blood and dust, with the sword still in
our hand. This is the path Jesus walked before us . . .

For Reflection:

1. Have you ever thought, "I just need to replace my sin with Jesus"?
Although theologically correct, how does this view miss the main problem
with idolatry?

2. How does the hope for a total deliverance, in which temptation is completely eradicated and obedience is no longer costly, reveal the heart of our idolatry?

3. In what ways do your idols deliver faster? How does it feel to have to wait on God and not take matters into your own hands? Where can you see God's purpose in allowing you to suffer with temptation?

DAY 3: FOLLOWING JESUS INTO THE MESS

How do you gauge God's goodness? For most of us, we measure it by the tangible, earthly blessings we receive from him—"I have a great wife and kids"; "I love my job"; "My business is successful." Sometimes it's more personal, but the issues are the same—"My kids were in rebellion, but now they're walking with the Lord"; "God saved my marriage, despite my sexual sin"; "There could have been horrific fallout in my career because of my behavior, but God was merciful." The list goes on and on.

But do you hear the heart behind all this? God's goodness is based on what he's done for me lately. It's rooted in *my* experience of life and the feelings that result. There's no focus on who *God* is, and what he's accomplished for me in Christ.

Jesus lived in a radically different way. Think about it: Jesus' life went from bad to worse. He was born into shame—seemingly an illegitimate child. People listened to his teaching, but wanted to exploit him to their own ends. In John 6, after the feeding of the five thousand, Jesus challenges that they're only seeking him because their bellies were filled. He was rejected by his people, rebuked by his family, betrayed with a kiss, deserted by his disciples, falsely accused in a sham court, then mocked, brutally beaten, and killed by pagans. But to the end, he clung to the Father, never wavering in his trust that the Father was good and faithful.

The Scriptures teach that Jesus' suffering was necessary. Read the following passages:

> For it was fitting that he, for whom and by whom all things exist, in bringing many sons to glory, should make the founder of their salvation perfect through suffering. (Hebrews 2:10)

> In the days of his flesh, Jesus offered up prayers and supplications, with loud cries and tears, to him who was able to save him from death, and he was heard because of his reverence. Although he was a son, he learned obedience through what he suffered. (Hebrews 5:7–8)

Is that hard for you to take in theologically? Wasn't Jesus always perfect? Wasn't he always obedient? What is the author of Hebrews talking about?

C. S. Lewis said, "Everyone feels benevolent if nothing happens to be annoying him at the moment."[19] In the same vein, I once heard someone comment, "People are like tea bags—you never know what you've got until you put them in hot water." If Jesus had lived an easy life, how would he have demonstrated the truth of his divinity and perfection? We know he was perfect because of how he suffered. His glory shining through his suffering revealed a life radically different than the world had ever seen.

In witnessing his death, the hard-bitten Roman centurion who had probably overseen the crucifixion of hundreds of men declared, "Truly this was the Son of God!" (Matthew 27:54). He had seen lots of men die, but never like this. Instead of pleading for mercy, raging against his enemies, or cursing God, Jesus willingly laid down his life. He hung on the cross crying out to God as Father, pleading for mercy on those who were killing him. This was a radically different life. His obedience and perfection were revealed through his suffering.

What does that mean for us? How is it helpful to know that Jesus learned obedience and was made perfect through suffering? Consider the following passages:

> Therefore he had to be made like his brothers in every respect, so that he might become a merciful and faithful high priest in the service of God, to make propitiation for the sins of the people. For because he himself has suffered when tempted, he is able to help those who are being tempted. (Hebrews 2:17–18)

> For we do not have a high priest who is unable to sympathize with our weaknesses, but one who in every respect has been tempted as we are, yet without sin. Let us then with confidence draw near to the throne of grace, that we may receive mercy and find grace to help in time of need. (Hebrews 4:15–16)

As we discussed in Week 7, Jesus knows exactly what you need. He is able to help you because he went through all these things too. He has been tempted just like us in every respect. Sometimes it's hard to get our minds around this reality. Think of the things you've done or been tempted to do—the ones that fill you with the most shame. Jesus knows what it's like to be tempted in that way. And because he endured the crucifixion as our atoning sacrifice, he even knows the horrible guilt and shame that go along with those acts, though he was never guilty of perpetrating them personally. Jesus knows poignantly and personally the ways that you suffer in your struggle against sin.

And here's the glorious hope: He suffered victoriously! Jesus isn't like an accountability partner, who struggles in exactly the same way so he can be empathetic with your struggle but can't offer any real hope because he's bogged down in his own mess. Jesus is truly the Wonderful Counselor because he's experienced the exact same trials—he *can* empathize—but he overcame them, so that he knows exactly what you need to be victorious.

Maybe you're thinking, "Okay, but Jesus was God. How can he possibly really understand my struggle? It wasn't possible for him to fail." Yes, Jesus was going to be successful in his mission to deliver us from sin and death. But we tend to focus on only half of his nature: The fact that he was 100% divine. But Scripture makes clear that he was also 100% human at the same time. "So that two whole, perfect, and distinct natures, the Godhead and the manhood, were inseparably joined together in one person, without conversion, composition, or confusion. Which person is very God, and very man, yet one Christ, the only Mediator between God and man."[20]

Those making the "But he was God" argument are losing sight of the reality of Christ's complete humanity. Although Scripture constrains me from saying that the purposes of God were ever "hanging in the balance," Jesus' suffering was nevertheless real. He really was hungry in the desert. Satan's offer to hand over the kingdoms of the world without the cross really was appealing. He sweated real drops of blood in the garden of Gethsemane. He truly agonized over his fate. The fact that his conclusion was never in doubt doesn't negate the reality of Jesus' suffering with temptation. His pleading with the Father was real, reflecting a heart in genuine turmoil. If you dismiss all this with "But he was God," you're cutting off your own way of escape! Listen again to Hebrews 2:18: "For because he himself has suffered when tempted, he is able to help those who are being tempted." Don't neglect the very real help Jesus offers you.

For Reflection:

1. What positive examples of suffering have you seen? How has God used suffering in your life (or with others you know) to ultimately bring about something good?

2. How do the passages about Jesus being perfected and learning obedience through suffering fit with your expectation of the Christian life? Explain.

3. What difference does it make that Jesus suffered victoriously? How can you be encouraged that he both understands your struggle and offers the strength and grace you need—because he not only was tempted in the same way but suffered victoriously?

DAY 4: NOT ALONE IN THE BATTLE

In Section 2, we examined the work of Christ and the reality that he is our conquering King, victoriously seated at the right hand of the Father—a position of power and authority. Although he has left us here for the "mop-up operation," he hasn't abandoned us. Even now he fights for and with us. He hasn't left us alone in the battle. The Christian life is not, "We're 100% dependent on God to get us into the kingdom, but then it's on us to work it all out." Scripture teaches that we are utterly dependent on him, from start to finish.

Jesus is the priest who intercedes for us. The writer of Hebrews works hard to demonstrate that Jesus is radically different, and better, than any who preceded him—angels, Moses, all other priests. After discussing how every other priest was limited both by personal sin and the finiteness of life, the writer concludes, "Consequently, he is able to save to the uttermost those who draw near to God through him, since he always lives to make intercession for them" (Hebrews 7:25). Jesus lives forever making intercession for his people.

I love how Romans 8:26 describes it: "Likewise the Spirit helps us in our weakness. For we do not know what to pray for as we ought, but the Spirit himself intercedes for us with groanings too deep for words." Apparently we don't even know how to pray correctly! The passage goes on: "Who is to condemn? Christ Jesus is the one who died—more than that, who was raised—who is at the right hand of God, who indeed is interceding for us" (Romans 8:34). Jesus and the Spirit continually intercede for us before the throne of our Father. The entire Godhead is passionately engaged with the intricacies of our lives, working behind the scenes on our redemption.

We need to be very careful to allow truth to dictate our response. So often we live by feelings, as if our experiences and emotions are the final judge of truth. While it might not feel as if God is carrying you along, he is. You receive genuine spiritual vitality through the ongoing, day-to-day, moment-by-moment intercession of Jesus and the Spirit. Further, Jesus has bound himself to us.

Maybe you wish Jesus were still physically present. You wish you could reach out and touch him, but at the resurrection he challenged Mary Magdalene, "Do not cling to me, for I have not yet ascended to the Father" (John 20:17). Jesus said it was *better* for him to ascend to heaven and send his Spirit. While on earth, Jesus was restricted to a single point on the globe. Now, by his Spirit, he is universally present with his people. And he has united himself to us. Listen to the wonder in the following passage:

> I do not ask for these only, but also for those who will believe in me through their word, that they may all be one, just as you, Father, are in me, and I in you, that they also may be in us, so that the world may believe that you have sent me. The glory that you have given me I have given to them, that they may be one even as we are one, I in them and you in me, that they may become perfectly one, so that the world may know that you sent me and loved them even as you loved me. (John 17:20–23)

After praying for the disciples, Jesus prays for all of us who believe—not only that we would be united as Christians, but that we would be united to him and the Father, just as they are one. We are included in the intimacy of the Godhead! Jesus declares that the Father loves us even as he loves Jesus. He describes our relationship in even more poignant language earlier in John:

> I am the true vine, and my Father is the vinedresser. Every branch of mine that does not bear fruit he takes away, and every branch that does bear fruit he prunes, that it may bear more fruit. Already you are clean because of the word that I have spoken to you. Abide in me, and I in you. As the branch cannot bear fruit by itself, unless it abides in the vine, neither can you, unless you abide in me. I am the vine; you are the branches. Whoever abides in me and I in him, he it is that bears much fruit, for apart from me you can do nothing. If anyone does not abide in me he is thrown away like a branch and withers; and the branches are gathered, thrown into the fire, and burned. (John 15:1–6)

Using an agricultural metaphor his hearers would have readily understood, Jesus describes his relationship to us and with the Father as a vine to its branches, with God as the vinedresser. We only bear fruit as we are connected to Jesus. Meditate on this reality: As a vine with its branches, Jesus has so completely joined himself to us that his life flows through us. Our union means his infinite power is available to us. Listen to how Paul describes this reality at work in believers:

> And what is the immeasurable greatness of his power toward us who believe, according to the working of his great might that he worked in Christ when he raised him from the dead and seated him at his right hand in the heavenly places. . . . (Ephesians 1:19–20)

> Now to him who is able to do far more abundantly than all that we ask or think, according to the power at work within us, to him be glory in the church and in Christ Jesus throughout all generations, forever and ever. Amen. (Ephesians 3:20–21)

The resurrection power that raised Jesus from the dead is at work in us, "able to do far more abundantly than all we ask or think." God gave us incredible imaginations, yet he's saying that he's able to do infinitely beyond what we can imagine. He has not left us alone in this battle—he offers us glorious power that is beyond our ability to comprehend!

For Reflection:

1. How does it make you feel to hear that you don't even know how to pray right? Does it encourage you because you know you're a mess, or discourage you because you'd like to believe you're more together than that? Explain.

2. When have you been encouraged to discover that someone was praying for you? What difference should it make, then, that Jesus and the Spirit are continually interceding for you—groaning for your soul?

3. How would your struggle with sexual sin be transformed if you understood how fully God's power was truly available to you? How can being united to Jesus impact your battle against sin?

DAY 5: GETTING VIOLENT

We need to be ruthless in battling our flesh. Scripture says "Put to death therefore what is earthly in you: sexual immorality, impurity, passion, evil desire, and covetousness, which is idolatry" (Colossians 3:5). Look at that list again. It's not surprising that every part of it fits with our sexual sin in some way. We are in a battle for our souls.

In Week 7, we talked about the reality of spiritual warfare. If you're skeptical, just start battling your sin and see the opportunities to fall back that seem to come out of nowhere. One man in our ministry had to stop and fix a flat tire on the expressway; a car went by, and the driver threw a porn magazine out the window right next to him. Another brother shared how he struggled with his computer; his accountability partner came over and locked it down. Then he struggled with TV; again, his buddy put on safeguards. Then he looked out the window and saw that the guy in the apartment across the alley was watching porn on his large-screen TV.

There is a battle raging, and we must be ruthless. The power of Christ at work in us doesn't passively carry us along. Our growth in grace is 100% the work of God and 100% our participation in that work. Listen to Paul's descriptions of this dynamic:

> Therefore, my beloved, as you have always obeyed, so now, not only as in my presence but much more in my absence, work out your own salvation with fear and trembling, for it is God who works in you, both to will and to work for his good pleasure. (Philippians 2:12–13)

> For this I toil, struggling with all his energy that he powerfully works within me. (Colossians 1:29)

The Christian life is serious business. We're to work out our salvation with fear and trembling. Paul is toiling and struggling—the verb in the original Greek evokes the idea of wrestling—but it is Jesus' energy at work within him. It's hard for us to understand this, but both aspects—our striving and Jesus' power in us—are equally true at the same time.

The devil doesn't want you to embrace this truth. For a long time he had you convinced that "resistance was futile." Failure was inevitable. This is a lie from the pit of hell. Christ is risen, and has poured his Spirit out upon you. You are more than a conqueror. The devil can bully you and lie to you, but when you resist he must flee from you (see James 4:7). We're challenged to take our stand against him, with the promise that we can stand firm in the full armor of God (see Ephesians 6:10–20).

Remember: battling temptation will be *hard*. But 1 Corinthians 10:13 says, "No temptation has overtaken you that is not common to man. God is faithful, and he will not let you be tempted beyond your ability, but with the temptation he will also provide the way of escape, that you may be able to endure it." You are not alone in the temptations you face. Other brothers are dealing with the same struggles. And God will be faithful to you. Jesus' is the victor who has suffered all the temptations you face victoriously so he knows the way of escape. But don't miss the conclusion: an escape is given "that you may be able to *endure*" the temptation. It won't be easy, but victory over temptation is glorious!

Are you ready to go to any lengths to be free from sin? Will you live without the Internet? Without cable TV? Will you move out of the neighborhood that is a constant source of temptation? What violent steps is God calling you to take to be victorious in this battle?

For Reflection:

1. Where do you need to get violent with sexual sin in your life? What sacrifices do you need to make in order to honor God with your sexuality?

2. Where do you need to get back in the fight? Do you have a hidden cache of porn in your closet or computer, or other objects hidden for sinful purposes? What specifically do you need to get rid of?

3. Where are you leaving the back door cracked open for sin—an unprotected computer or cable TV in a secluded area of the house, keeping someone's number, not changing *your* number? Are you ruthless in addressing each area, and bringing others into the fight with you? Be specific.

WEEK 12:
RUTHLESS HONESTY

KEY CONCEPT: All of us know the experience of guilt and shame, thus we live in fear of exposure. We do everything possible to keep our sin hidden. However, the Bible declares that everything hidden in the dark will be brought into the light; therefore, as Christians, we are called to walk in the light. We don't need to be perfect, just honest. Confessing our struggle with sin to other men demonstrates the reality of our faith. This is crucial because how we speak reveals the allegiance of our hearts. The irony of our hiding is that it guarantees we will stay stuck in sin. God promises that if we're willing to risk being honest with others, we'll experience the blessing of genuine relationships and find the thing we've been desperately longing for—increasing freedom from our struggle with sin!

DAY 1: FEARING EXPOSURE

All of us live in fear of exposure. We don't want the worst things about us to be known. As discussed earlier, we posture and wear masks. We establish elaborate façades and hide behind our good deeds. This refusal to be truly known and exposed keeps us stuck in our sin more than anything else. Listen to how Jesus described our hiding:

> And this is the judgment: the light has come into the world, and
> people loved the darkness rather than the light because their deeds
> were evil. For everyone who does wicked things hates the light
> and does not come to the light, lest his works should be exposed.
> But whoever does what is true comes to the light, so that it may
> be clearly seen that his works have been carried out in God. (John
> 3:19–21)

All of us hate this. We all fear exposure. Even if you're an exhibitionist, you know this is true. An exhibitionist is willing to expose his body on *his* terms—according to who he wants to see it and when. But there is a radical difference between the exposure of our outward, physical selves and the dark depths of our souls laid bare.

None of us relish being known for the worst things about us. But the scary truth is that all of us will eventually be completely exposed. The Bible is very clear on this point. Our lives will be laid bare before the only One who truly matters. Consider these passages:

> Nothing is covered up that will not be revealed, or hidden that will
> not be known. Therefore whatever you have said in the dark shall be
> heard in the light, and what you have whispered in private rooms
> shall be proclaimed on the housetops. (Luke 12:2–3).

> Therefore do not pronounce judgment before the time, before
> the Lord comes, who will bring to light the things now hidden in
> darkness and will disclose the purposes of the heart. Then each one
> will receive his commendation from God. (1 Corinthians 4:5)

Do these passages terrify you? Growing up in a fundamentalist church, I remember hearing that my life would be shown before every person who ever lived on a *huge* outdoor screen, one hundred times the size of a drive-in movie. This was a terrifying thought to a kid who was exposed to porn as a child at a friend's house and discovered masturbation at a young age. Although none of us know what God has in store, I doubt it's that. In fact, this seems to be a manipulative ploy, trying to bring about obedience by exploiting our fear of man.

But this much is clear: Our lives will be exposed, either in this life or the next. Exposure in this life will be deeply humbling, but we have God's promise that those who believe in him will never be put to shame (see Romans 10:11). We don't have a choice whether or not exposure will happen—it definitely will—but we can either be exposed now for our good and not be put to shame, or be forcefully exposed on the final day as a fraud, facing eternal shame. As we'll explore further tomorrow, the only way out of our mess with sexual sin is to step boldly into the light, believing God's promise to cover and protect those who trust him.

For Reflection:

1. Has God ever forced your sexual sin into the light? What was that experience like? Though initially painful, how have you seen God's goodness in this?

2. In what ways have you been blessed by allowing others to know the worst about you? When have you been terrified to share about your behaviors, only to experience relief once it was over?

3. Along with the fear of exposure is the weight of carrying the burden alone, maintaining the façade, etc. What would it be like to be free of those burdens?

DAY 2: WALKING IN THE LIGHT

Although we long to be victorious in our struggle with sexual sin, our refusal to let others in—to let them really know us—is the very thing keeping us stuck. We say we believe that Jesus takes our sin and clothes us with his righteousness, but our life of hiding reveals the doubt in our soul. We're going to take some time unpacking the following passage:

> This is the message we have heard from him and proclaim to you, that God is light, and in him is no darkness at all. If we say we have fellowship with him while we walk in darkness, we lie and do not practice the truth. But if we walk in the light, as he is in the light, we have fellowship with one another, and the blood of Jesus his Son cleanses us from all sin. If we say we have no sin, we deceive ourselves, and the truth is not in us. If we confess our sins, he is faithful and just to forgive us our sins and to cleanse us from all unrighteousness. If we say we have not sinned, we make him a liar, and his word is not in us. (1 John 1:5–10)

We've spent a fair bit of time looking at the reality that we deceive others—the blatant ways we hide our behavior from spouse, family, close friends, and how we also subtly do it through our posturing and public good works. All this hiding and posturing prevents us from growing in intimacy with others. But John highlights a further problem: We deceive ourselves. In addiction circles, there's a joke that addicts like to spend time on the river De-nial. We have a huge problem with downplaying our struggle with sin, making excuses for what we're doing. Yet on some level, we're completely blind to what we do.

I have a friend who struggled with calling sex-chat lines, so as an accountability measure his cell-phone bill came to me. One day as we sat down to look at the bill, I asked him how many calls he'd made that month. He guessed three or four. We went over the bill line by line and discovered he had made *sixteen* calls—four times more than he thought! He didn't intend to lie to me. He knew he couldn't deceive me. I was holding the bill in my hand. Yet, he deceived me because he deceived himself.

Although not all self-deceit is so blatant, this is an issue for all of us. And again, it points to our need to have brothers in our lives who are allowed to be intrusive. We only overcome our self-deceit as we actively let others into our lives, and let them see what's going on inside our heads and hearts.

John proposes that, as opposed to those who walk in darkness (and prefer it because their deeds are evil), we're welcomed to walk in the light. It doesn't mean we live lives that are pristine, but lives that are exposed. John challenges us to be honest. Every believer struggles with sin. The question is not, "Do you sin?" but rather, "What do you *do* when you sin?" This passage calls us to a life of exposure instead of a life of hiding. John's concern is that people in the church are not living honestly with one another. They are posing and playing a Christian game. He calls on us to stop deceiving others and ourselves, and start being honest about the real brokenness we have.

For Reflection:

1. When have you realized you were self-deceived? How did you discover it? Who in your life today is willing to challenge your self-deceit?

2. What does it mean to you to walk in the light? How have you understood that calling in the past?

3. How much hiding still occurs in your life? Do you have secrets you plan to take to your grave? How do you think those secrets affect your closest relationships?

DAY 3: THE "FORMULA" FOR CHANGE

You may have noticed that Scripture doesn't offer ten easy steps to holy living. Apparently God isn't into self-help formulas. But in 1 John 1:7, God *is* offering us a formula of sorts—honest confession = fellowship + freedom from sin. If we're willing to be honest with others about our struggle with sin, God promises we'll experience genuine fellowship with others, and the blood of Jesus will cleanse us from sin.

Many of us have memorized 1 John 1:9 and can rattle it off without missing a beat. Furthermore, I suspect you've viewed that verse purely as a transaction between you and Jesus. It's not. We miss the connection with verse 7: "But if we walk in the light, as he is in the light, we have fellowship with one another, and the blood of Jesus his Son cleanses us from all sin." The entire thrust of the passage is about corporate confession. It's a promise from God that if you confess your sin to your brothers, then, as verse 9 promises, he will "be faithful and just to forgive us our sins and to cleanse us from all unrighteousness."

John goes to great pains to point out the reality of our deception. We're called to walk *in* the light because we're being called *out* of darkness and hiding. Consider also Proverbs 28:13: "Whoever conceals his transgressions will not prosper, but he who confesses and forsakes them will obtain mercy." Who do we conceal our sin from? The God who knows all? We can't. But we can, and do, hide our sin from each other. John's saying that must stop.

God has always called his people to corporate confession. Consider the Old Testament sacrificial system. It's a pretty public thing to walk into the temple courtyard with your lamb saying, "We've got to kill this thing because of what I did last night." That's radically public confession. The ministry of John the Baptist was founded on people publicly confessing their sin and receiving a baptism of repentance. Likewise, James 5:16 prescribes, "Therefore, confess your sins to one another and pray for one another, that you may be healed. The prayer of a righteous person has great power as it is working." The only way to find freedom from sexual sin is to be committed to ruthless honesty with others.

All of us have tried to overcome our battle with sin on our own. We've fasted, prayed, memorized Scripture. Some have even tried a homespun version of old-fashioned shock therapy—snapping rubber bands against their wrists with every lustful thought, desperately trying to create a psychological aversion. We've served the church and woke before the sun for quiet times with God. Nothing has worked. Why? Because we're trying to do it without ruthless honesty. We're not living the Christian life the way God says it must be lived. An Aston Martin V12 Vantage is an amazing car (and costs more than my house). But it only gets up to 190 mph if you put high octane gas in the tank. If the Vantage has a gas tank filled with maple syrup, you'd be better off in my '93 Subaru Legacy with more than 190,000 miles—which goes from zero to sixty in 1.3 minutes. The car's amazing capabilities are only unleashed when you operate it correctly. The Christian life is the same. There will be no power in your life to overcome sin until you follow God's formula.

Jesus reserved his harshest words for religious hypocrites. And the truth is, all of us have had the experience of living like hypocrites. The Greek word for "hypocrite" refers to actors in a drama, and illustrates how we posture and pretend. I know there are times when you've felt like a hypocrite, publicly professing one thing and being a very different person in private. How do you overcome hypocrisy? Honesty! You must be willing to be exposed.

One disclaimer to those alone in the struggle: The call to corporate confession doesn't mean get up on Sunday morning during the worship service and spill your guts. Your confession must be "public," but you need to exercise wisdom. Begin with your pastor. Ask him to suggest others who can walk with you. Again, if you're in a church where you can't talk to your pastor about these issues, you're in the wrong church! But as I also said in Week 9, first take the risk and *try* talking to him.

For Reflection:

1. What different formulas or self-help strategies have you used, trying to overcome your sexual sin? How have they helped? In what ways have they fallen short?

2. What does it feel like to live as a hypocrite? When have you been challenged with the importance of ruthless honesty? Do you believe this is the only way you'll find freedom? Why or why not?

3. Have you ever been a part of a church or group that was committed to corporate confession of personal sin? How have you benefited from sharing your struggle with others?

DAY 4: THE BLESSINGS OF HONESTY

God doesn't call us to hard things just to make us suffer. The call to ruthless honesty comes with the promise of blessing. One of the blessings promised in 1 John 1:7 is that you'll experience genuine fellowship with others. What does this mean?

You know what it's like to walk into church on a Sunday morning with your heart aching, and just putting on the plastic smile and playing the Christian game. You end up leaving in greater pain than when you came. Any benefit from the sermon, worship, the Lord's Supper, seems to evaporate as you engage in one superficial conversation after another on your way out the door. It's brutal not to be known, to suffer in silence with your sin and heartache. Consider how different the experience would be if you pulled a brother aside before entering the sanctuary, shared the state of your soul, and asked him to pray for you to believe in God's promises—*then* entered into worship. You would leave encouraged, rejoicing in the goodness of God.

Similarly, I know you've had the experience of giving a veiled confession. Eventually the pain of wearing a mask was too great and you ventured a partial confession, maybe saying lust was a problem, but not divulging the depths of your behavior. The brother tried to encourage you, but it didn't really help. Why? You weren't being completely honest. The whole time he's reminding you of the truth of God's love and mercy in Christ, you're thinking, "But if he really knew what I was dealing with, he wouldn't be saying this right now. He'd be gathering the elders to excommunicate me!"

The fact is, a brother's encouragement isn't very encouraging unless he knows *specifically* how you're struggling. You will not be encouraged, nor have genuine fellowship, until people really know you. You must risk coming into the light, because you can only be truly encouraged by others if they know the places where you're discouraged.

Conversely, it's glorious to meet with a brother when you're completely discouraged, to put the worst stuff of your soul on the table, and still be reminded of God's goodness and mercy. Fellowship is intended to strengthen our souls and safeguard our hearts. Listen to this exhortation from Hebrews 3:12–13, "See to it, brothers, that none of you has a sinful, unbelieving heart that turns away from the living God. But encourage one another daily, as long as it is called Today, so that none of you may be hardened by sin's deceitfulness" (NIV). This passage prescribes daily fellowship as a means of staving off the deceitfulness of our hearts, the hardening effects of sin. We need others to remind us of the truth of the gospel when we're struggling with despair.

Where will you turn? Some men, when confronted by the problems in their marriage, the disappointments in their career, the lack of a spouse, the persistence of temptation, financial stress, etc., turn to others in the face of despair. When they struggle to believe the truth of God's presence in their lives, his commitment to them, and the reality of his mercy in Christ, they reach out to someone else to remind them. Others give in to despair and seek comfort wherever they can find it. For most of us, that means returning to our sexual sin of choice. Ruthless honesty about the reality of our unbelief and fellowship with one another are tangible, practical means that God uses to work his power in us through his people, to enable us to overcome our struggle with sin.

The second blessing promised in 1 John 1:7 is that when we walk in the light God will cleanse us from our sin. This Greek word is used elsewhere in the New Testament to describe people cleansed from leprosy. It is a present active indicative verb suggesting ongoing action. This is what John is saying: Do you want to be free from the sin that dogs you today? Ruthless honesty is the road. If you practice this, it unleashes the promises of God in your life. It puts feet on the gospel. It's one thing to say you trust Jesus, but something entirely different to demonstrate a reckless, radical trust in his promises by exposing the worst things about yourself to your brothers. It is a fragrant sacrifice, a powerful demonstration of love and trust in your deliverer. As we'll see more fully in Week 14, as we humble ourselves God gives us more grace. There's nothing more humbling than being known at our worst. It unleashes the power of the gospel.

Think about it this way: our tongue demonstrates a fundamental allegiance. Jesus said the devil is the father of lies (John 8:44). When we actively practice deceit—whether it's blatant deception or subtly withholding important information—our lives demonstrate an allegiance to the deceiver of the whole world and his domain of darkness.[21]

But if we speak truth—if we're honest about our struggle with sin and freely disclose our ongoing failures—we demonstrate an allegiance to the One who is truth incarnate, whose kingdom is a kingdom of light. Practicing ruthless honesty is decisively turning away from Satan and his lies to embrace

Jesus and all his promises. It would be hard to put it more strongly: Ruthless honesty demonstrates the reality of saving faith.

For Reflection:

1. Describe a time when you suffered in silence with your sin. What did that feel like? What was it like to be around other Christians?

2. Describe an experience of genuine fellowship and encouragement. How does this contrast with what happens when you give a veiled confession?

3. Does it make sense that honesty unleashes the power of the gospel? Why or why not? Where do you need to take a clear stand against the enemy and demonstrate your love for Christ through the power of confession?

DAY 5: FREE TO BE RUTHLESSLY HONEST

Ruthless honesty demonstrates the reality of saving faith. It demonstrates an allegiance to Jesus who *is* truth, and publicly drives a stake in the ground for the sake of the gospel. To be known as a sinner in need of God's mercy—not in a generic sense, but with specificity—is to publicly claim Jesus as your Redeemer. Even though we all do this in some sense when we go forward at an altar call, get baptized, or take membership vows, there's something profound about publicly confessing specific, shameful sins in our lives. It makes no sense apart from the gospel. Unless you're certain that your sins are covered by the blood of Christ, you'll hide the truth about yourself and present a façade to the world.

But the gospel frees us to be ruthlessly honest. How? In Week 9 we looked at the two truths of the gospel—Jesus' need to die shows that we're far worse than we ever imagined, but at the same time shows that we're more loved and cherished than we'd ever dare hope! The sacrifice of Jesus is proof of our Father's profound love for us. It demonstrates his radical, self-giving commitment to be reconciled to the creatures he made and loves. Now, we are invited to bask in his love. Because of Jesus' atoning work on the cross, the only one who truly matters in the entire universe forgives, accepts, and delights in us.

And it goes deeper. C. S. Lewis, in his sermon "The Weight of Glory," describes heaven as a place where we'll perfectly receive God's love and affirmation, hearing, "Well done, good and faithful servant" without any hint of arrogance. He concludes, "In the end that Face which is the delight or the terror of the universe must be turned upon each of us either with one expression or with the other, either conferring glory inexpressible or inflicting shame that can never be cured or disguised."[22] All of us have poignantly experienced shame. Because of Jesus, God's promise is that for all eternity we'll worship and glorify him—and that he will glorify us. Consider the declaration of 2 Corinthians 4:16–18:

> So we do not lose heart. Though our outer self is wasting away, our inner nature is being renewed day by day. For this slight momentary affliction is preparing for us an eternal weight of glory beyond all comparison, as we look not to the things that are seen but to the things that are unseen. For the things that are seen are transient, but the things that are unseen are eternal.

The one who created all things, who fills the universe, has glory in store for us. It is glory that we can't begin to comprehend, a weight of glory that only our resurrected bodies can endure. Meditate on the wonder of that for a moment. Despite your guilt and all the behaviors of your past and present that fill you with shame, the Creator of the universe has glory in store for you! He promises to bring us safely through all the trials of this life, shape us through them to more and more resemble Jesus, and ultimately use them to make eternity even more wondrous. The suffering we're called to endure is preparing us for pleasure and glory "beyond all comparison."

God's approval, and his covering of our sins in Christ Jesus, gives us the freedom to be ruthlessly honest. When we embrace the truth of the gospel, we are freed from shame and the slavery of others' approval. There's nothing more important for you right now than to grasp the wonder of God's love for you, so that you "may have strength to comprehend with all the saints what is the breadth and length and height and depth, and to know the love of Christ that surpasses knowledge, that you may be filled with all the fullness of God" (Ephesians 3:18–19).

There's probably nothing in this life more wonderful than being in love. God wants us to learn that our experience of falling in love in this broken world is a dim reflection of the glorious reality of his love for us. Isaiah 62:5 says, "For as a young man marries a young woman, so shall your sons marry you, and as the bridegroom rejoices over the bride, so shall your God rejoice over you." Our experience of God's love and delight will continue to grow for all eternity. Resting in the certainty of his love and our complete acceptance in Christ frees us from the tyranny of our fear of man, and enables us to honestly confess our struggles and thus unleash the power of the gospel in our lives.

I love how Paul describes this dynamic in his life. Likely confronted with a physical infirmity that he referred to as a thorn in his flesh, Paul pleaded repeatedly for Jesus to deliver him to no avail. Instead Paul recounts, "But he said to me, 'My grace is sufficient for you, for my power is made perfect in weakness.' Therefore I will boast all the more gladly of my weaknesses, so that the power of Christ may rest upon me" (2 Corinthians 12:9). Did you catch his conclusion? There is a direct connection between our willingness to be exposed (boasting in our weakness) and the power of Christ being poured out on us. As we'll examine at length in Week 14, when we humble ourselves God gives us more grace.

For Reflection:

1. When was the last time you experienced the joy of God's forgiveness—the wonder that he loves you enough to offer up Jesus for you? What was it like?

2. If you could gaze into Jesus' eyes at this moment, what do you think you would see? Think also about the right "Sunday school" answer—that Jesus is looking at you in love. What prevents you from living as if this were really true?

3. What does it mean to you that God has an "eternal weight of glory" in store for you? Do you believe that God looks forward to glorifying you? How would your life change if you could fully grasp this hope?

WEEK 13:
REDEFINING ACCOUNTABILITY

KEY CONCEPT: There's a lot of talk in the church about accountability. Too often accountability is reduced to sin management, a list of don'ts to avoid. However, good relationships with other men will push us to become the men God created us to be, taking seriously and growing in applying the two Great Commandments to love God and others. This includes ruthlessly stamping out our sexual sin, but it is so much more. Like lifting weights with a buddy, we need men who'll push us spiritually beyond our perceived limits. We need others' eyes to help us see ourselves rightly and understand the motivations behind our sexual sin.

Many of us have had negative experiences with letting other men in, but it's essential to overcoming our struggle with sexual sin. It reminds us of the structure of the universe: We are answerable for our lives.

DAY 1: ACCOUNTABILITY IS GOOD

I hate the word *accountability*. It makes people cringe. Many of us have had bad experiences with it. Nonetheless, accountability is something we all need. It provides the context for ruthless honesty, without which you will not overcome your sin.

Here's another word for it, though it's not as catchy—answerability. We need accountability because it reminds us of a fundamental truth of our existence: We're answerable for our lives. We're not autonomous. In past weeks we looked at our propensity to overlook this truth, believing that we can get away with our behaviors and that God will just forgive us anyway. The truth is: We *will* be called to account on the Last Day. Accountability is crucial because it keeps us mindful of the structure of the universe.

I love the story of the Roman centurion in Luke 7:1–10. The centurion's servant is sick, so he sends messengers to ask Jesus to heal him. But the centurion's message has a wild conclusion: "For I too am a man set under authority, with soldiers under me: and I say to one, 'Go,' and he goes; and to another, 'Come,' and he comes; and to my servant, 'Do this,' and he does it" (Luke 7:7–8).

What's Jesus' response? He praises the man, saying he hasn't seen such faith in all of Israel. Why? The centurion demonstrates that he understands how the universe works. He lives under authority. He knows autonomy is a lie. He's drawing connections between his professional life in the Roman military and the ultimate reality that God rules over all. This believing centurion knows he's answerable to higher authorities, both professionally and spiritually.

Accountability, when done properly, reminds us of this ultimate truth. We are all God's servants, who ultimately must give an account. As we come before our brothers week after week to account for ourselves, it's an opportunity to reflect on the reality that we are rehearsing week after week for the final day.

A quick word here: If you're married, your wife should *never* be your accountability partner. This doesn't mean that God isn't calling you to ruthless honesty with her—he is!—but the accountability dynamic is incredibly unhealthy to a marriage. Nothing could be further from God's design for marriage than to play "cops and robbers" with your wife. She needs you to have men in your life asking you the hard questions, so she knows that she won't have to.

Accountability with other men will help heal your marriage. Many wives badger their husbands with questions for a long time after sexual sin has been confessed. They want a full accounting of finances, time, etc. Often their demands are fully warranted, and the depth of a husband's repentance can be gauged by his willingness to live a life of radical openness. Understand, your wife is so wounded and betrayed by your sin that she's terrified of being deceived again. Rebuilding trust and becoming vulnerable to even more pain is overwhelming and often results in a perpetual game of "20 Questions." Good accountability gives your wife peace of mind and enables her to begin trusting again. Knowing that someone else is handling this responsibility frees both of you to focus on rebuilding your relationship. She needs you to have it as much as you do. And your marriage will be in a much better place if your interactions aren't constantly marked by her questioning.

For Reflection:

1. Describe your experiences with accountability. Have you ever seen it as a reminder of the structure of the universe? How might this perspective change the dynamic and your perceptions about accountability?

2. How else do you battle against an autonomous mindset? How does it impact your relationships?

3. If married, has your wife served as your accountability partner? How has that impacted your marriage? How might it benefit your wife if she knew other men were asking you the hard questions?

DAY 2: ACCOUNTABILITY: THE BASICS

Every man needs rigorous accountability, whether he struggles with sexual sin or not. We don't grow in the Christian life without intentional work and, because everything we've already discussed in Section 3 is true, that intentionality must include others. This means working through this book is just the beginning: you should plan on being a part of a small accountability group with other men for the rest of your life. Living the Christian life without deep, vital relationships with other Christian men is not following the call of Christ.

I suggest a group of at least three, but definitely not bigger than six or seven. Why the minimum? Because these relationships require saying hard things to each other and we're so resistant to hearing the truth about ourselves, it's helpful to hear the challenge from more than one person. We can still be dismissive of two people, but it's harder. As they used to say in Narcotics Anonymous, "If one person says you're a horse you can blow them off. If two people say it, you should look for a tail. But if three people say you're a horse—it's time to saddle up!" When hard things need to be said, a multitude of counselors is helpful. Further, in a one-on-one situation, we might be tempted toward placating and shrink back from giving the direct challenge that needs to be heard.

The reason for the upper limit is probably obvious. Any group larger than five or six men becomes a place that's too easy to hide in. Also, from a practical standpoint, meeting together takes way too much time.

It's ideal if the men you meet with come from diverse backgrounds and have different struggles. Every man doesn't need to be struggling with sin in the same way you are. They just need to know that they also have plenty of sin to repent of, and that the gospel is the same hope for all of you. If men know how to point one another to Jesus, they can walk with each other no matter how different their specific struggles are. In fact, having men who struggle with different things can help us take our eyes off ourselves and our own personal sin issues.

It's also helpful to have men at different levels of maturity in Christ. As long as the "mature" man is clinging to the gospel—rather than being a self-righteous Pharisee masquerading as mature, but blind to the heinousness of his pride and good works—there's a tremendous blessing to be gained from his years of walking with Christ and growing in grace. Why? One way that accountability often goes astray is by turning into "sin management." We all know where the *really* bad line is. As long as nobody crosses that and we maintain the sin status quo, it's okay. Having a truly mature Christian present reduces the likelihood of this dynamic occurring.

Too many of us view the Christian life as "cruise control." You merge on the obedience highway, get up to speed with all the surrounding vehicles and then . . . just cruise. Describing it this way, author Jerry Bridges says our faith should look more like NASCAR—screaming around the track, one with the machine and pushing it to the limit to get the wave of the checkered flag.[23] We need mature believers to keep us on track, to keep us from settling for sin management, and to spur us on to "win the prize."

In radical contrast to our typical approach to the Christian life and obedience, consider how Jesus describes the battle with our flesh:

> And if your hand or your foot causes you to sin, cut it off and throw
> it away. It is better for you to enter life crippled or lame than with
> two hands or two feet to be thrown into the eternal fire. And if your
> eye causes you to sin, tear it out and throw it away. It is better for
> you to enter life with one eye than with two eyes to be thrown into
> the hell of fire. (Matthew 18:8–9)

I don't believe Jesus actually intended every one of us to commit bodily injury. He's using the starkest description imaginable to jar us into seeing the importance of our obedience. The gravest matter in the universe is at stake— our eternal destiny. It's not that our obedience earns us points with God. Instead, like the truth-speaking we discussed last week, obedience is tangible fruit in our lives that shows that we truly believe the gospel.

I've been in accountability groups in the past that were in the sin-management category. They fed my pride (I made sure to stay well within the acceptable sin limit), and we failed to really point each other to Christ and to call one another to radical obedience. We were young and immature and desperately needed an older, wiser man to speak into our lives.

Although public confession is crucial, it's only the beginning. The intensity of the battle discussed in Week 11—the ruthless commitment to cut off whatever stands in our way—means these relationships are *supposed* to be challenging. Like Gollum in the *Lord of the Rings* trilogy, we don't want to let go of our "precious." We need to enter these relationships with the knowledge that it will be costly. If we're doing it right, not every meeting is going to end with a warm pat on the back!

There's a poignant picture of this reality in *All Quiet on the Western Front*. A group of young recruits arrive at the front, just in time for a massive bombardment. The shelling goes on continually for more than twenty-four hours. Huddled in the quaking dugout, cabin fever sets in. The recruits begin to lose it. One of them bolts out of the dugout and is immediately obliterated, hunks of flesh plastered to the side of the trench. Nevertheless, a few minutes later another starts inching toward the door. Two of the old hands grab him and literally pummel him to bring him to his senses. It only seems merciless; it's actually a form of severe mercy.[24] In the same way, we desperately need men in our lives who'll give us a spiritual beating when we're crazy and blind to our folly!

For Reflection:

1. Have you ever been in a "sin management" accountability group? How did this experience impact your soul?

2. In what ways do you operate on Christian cruise control? Do you *want* your Christian life to be like NASCAR? Explain.

3. How do you gauge what's okay regarding your use of entertainment, music, money? With whom do you tend to compare yourself?

4. Who in your life is willing to give you a spiritual beating (in love) when you need it? Are you pursuing an accountability relationship with that person currently? Why or why not?

DAY 3: PUTTING ON . . .

As you establish accountability, avoid an exhaustive, generic questionnaire for two reasons. First, the flesh will always find a loophole or invent some new vehicle for sin. Second, deep, intimate relationships are crucial for overcoming our struggles with sin; therefore, hearing "no" one hundred times doesn't enable you to know an individual on any deeper level—even if you go over the list for years!

Lots of those tedious lists of questions end with "Did you lie to me?" as if it's the perfect catch-all. The problem is, we are deeply deceiving and self-deceived people. Our hearts are unbelievably crafty at manipulating the truth. I've sat listening to husbands spin a situation in which the lies were blatant and weeks later are still convinced they were "technically" telling the truth—while their wives watch on in utter disbelief. After more than a decade of working with men struggling with sexual sin, I'm convinced that we'll never come up with a questionnaire that gets to the bottom of all the potential behaviors and still get you to work on time (or home for a decent night's sleep). We need a different approach.

A short list of five or six questions, tailored specifically to our individual struggles, is far more effective. And the questions need to be open-ended, requiring reflection, not simple yes-or-no answers. For example, if you know the daily commute has been a problem, rather than asking, "Did you stop at _____ while driving home from work this week?" a better question is, "How did you respond when you were driving by _____? What was going on inside of you?" One question allows an easy no; the other engages the heart. You must allow others to know the aspects of your soul that you've kept carefully hidden in the past. The questions need to be different for every individual, responding to the specifics of each personal struggle.

Further, accountability is frequently focused only on the negative, trying to find out if you committed this or that sin. But God doesn't call us to a vacuous place of absent sin. The call of the gospel is radical allegiance to our King. Scripture describes the transformation in us as putting off and putting on. We're to exchange our sinful behaviors for a life that increasingly reflects the glory of Jesus manifested in us. Ephesians 4:20–32 and Colossians 3:5–17 powerfully demonstrate how this exchange is to take place in our lives.

Therefore, good accountability always balances putting-off and putting-on questions. Our questions have to challenge us to become the men God created us to be. This includes challenges to put away sinful behaviors, but it also includes questions that reveal how we're becoming men who look more like Jesus. Our questions should help us gauge whether we're stagnant or nurturing the life of God in us.

In light of this deeper calling to grow into Christ-likeness, consider the following passage:

> Owe no one anything, except to love each other, for the one who
> loves another has fulfilled the law. For the commandments, "You
> shall not commit adultery, You shall not murder, You shall not steal,
> You shall not covet," and any other commandment, are summed up
> in this word: "You shall love your neighbor as yourself." Love does
> no wrong to a neighbor; therefore love is the fulfilling of the law.
>
> Besides this you know the time, that the hour has come for you to
> wake from sleep. For salvation is nearer to us now than when we first
> believed. The night is far gone; the day is at hand. So then let us cast
> off the works of darkness and put on the armor of light. Let us walk
> properly as in the daytime, not in orgies and drunkenness, not in sexual
> immorality and sensuality, not in quarreling and jealousy. But put on
> the Lord Jesus Christ, and make no provision for the flesh, to gratify its
> desires. (Romans 13:8–14)

The way to overcome sexual sin is through loving God and others, not developing behavioral modification techniques. Do you hear the hope in the passage? Salvation is near. The darkness is giving way as the new day dawns. We're invited to walk as citizens of the kingdom of light. And, as we'll examine further on Day 5, the most significant command is for us to "put on the Lord Jesus Christ," making "no provision for the flesh."

When opening your accountability time, it's best to begin with the positive, considering what it means to become the man God's calling you to be. Therefore, your first question should focus on developing your relationship with God. This will look different for each person. Some men never read the Bible. If you're one of them, then you need to start! Others have read through it every year for years, but it's become a static intellectual exercise, devoid of genuine communion with God. If that's you, spend more time praying than you do reading. I've challenged men to only read a handful of verses a day, but to pray over every line. Other men should be challenged to journal, spending time reflecting on their day and writing out prayers. So how do you figure out what *you* should be doing?

First, with others' help, identify the deficits in your relationship. Get together with your pastor or another leader in your church. Find out how they practice spiritual disciplines, nurture their prayer life, etc. Oswald Chambers has put it well, "When a man is born from above, the life of the Son of God begins in him, and he can either starve that life or nourish it."[25] A significant factor in our sexual idolatry is that at some point after conversion, we fall away from a vital, joyous relationship with God. We need brothers to directly challenge us to take our relationship with God seriously once again, then do everything we can to live moment by moment with God.

The next putting-on focus is your primary relationships. Carefully consider how you're doing loving the people God has placed in your life, especially those closest to you. (Thus, accountability begins with focusing on the positives of the two Great Commandments—to love God and to love others.) Again, this is going to look different for each person, not only in terms of relationships, but how love is expressed. The first focus should be on immediate family (if married) or housemates, then extended family, coworkers, neighbors, friends. And because God is committed to our sanctification, we all have people in our lives that are difficult to love. We desperately need brothers to hold our feet to the fire, challenging us to be the men God is calling us to be in those relationships! A couple of specific questions unique to your relationships are crucial. They need to target ways you can grow positively in loving your spouse, children, housemates, extended family, and friends. Be honest about the hardest person God has placed in your life, and prayerfully engage in a campaign of love toward that person. You'll be amazed how God changes your heart toward difficult people and by the ripple effects of grace that extend from you to others.

For Reflection:

1. How do you need to be encouraged to grow in your relationship with God—Bible reading, prayer, journaling, etc.? What would growth look like specifically in your case?

2. Who's the most difficult person for you to love right now? Do you believe God put him or her in your life for your good? What would it look like for you to have an agenda of love toward that person?

3. How would those closest to you rate your attention to their concerns? Are you willing to ask them for feedback on how you need to grow in your relationships? Why or why not?

DAY 4: PUTTING OFF . . .

Once we've looked at the putting-on of loving God and others, we're ready to check in on the dangerous places in our lives. We were warned in Romans 13:14 to "make no provision for the flesh, to gratify its desires." Historically, our modus operandi had been to do the exact opposite—work hard to make provision for our flesh as frequently as possible. We adjusted our calendars, manipulated our finances, and told lie upon lie in order to pave the way for our sin. Now, we begin to work toward undoing all that.

We must be willing to let our brothers ask intrusive questions. Remember, this is far deeper than a life-or-death issue; this is a battle with cosmic consequences. We need to take this seriously, because it is. Our sexuality reveals our spirituality. This doesn't mean salvation is based on your performance. James, after writing extensively about the fact that "faith apart from works is dead" (James 2:26), still acknowledges that "we all stumble in many ways" (James 3:2). Nonetheless, there should be a trajectory of becoming more Christlike and growing in grace—even if this initially means just being honest about our failures.

The questions should be specific to your struggle and open-ended. If your struggle is with Internet porn, there should be targeted questions such as, "Describe a time when you were tempted to go online this week. Did you give in?" You need to ask the bottom line on behaviors, but that can't be the only question. You might need to be asked several different questions about various behaviors, depending on your situation and the nature of your struggle. Obviously, the best approach is to be forthright from the beginning. Accountability is only as good as you want it to be. If you turn it into a game where you only speak the truth if you're asked the right question, you're wasting everyone's time.

Although we've looked at the reality that sexual sin is not primarily about lust, we need to be wary about the specific situations that create greater opportunities for sin. Most of us need accountability when we travel or if we're going to be without our families for any length of time. Business trips are the classic scenarios for infidelity. There's something about being away from home that makes us even more susceptible to the autonomy lie. Even going on a family vacation can be challenging—not just because you're seeing a lot of skin on the beach, but because the whole vacation attitude tends to be self-focused, causing our sin to thrive. Not to mention our demand that our vacation be a hassle-free good time, combined with the pressure to have fun given the cash outlay. Good accountability pays attention to both the special scenarios we face as well as the ebb and flow of daily living.

Further, accountability needs to identify the sin behind the sin. It is first and foremost a violation of the first commandment, an idol that replaces the Creator. In the face of frustration, loneliness, anxiety, disappointment, stress, etc., we're tempted to run to a false savior. Rather than collapsing on Christ, pouring out our hearts, and receiving his peace, we take matters into our own hands. There are times when temptation is like an ambush on a beautiful, sunny day, when everything is fine. Usually though, there are predictable patterns of behavior—sinful responses to the challenges of life in a fallen world. We need to grow in our knowledge of one another so we can begin to help each other see these patterns. Some guys struggling financially are going to be really tempted when it's time to pay the bills. Others face job pressures at different times, which increase temptation. For those of us who are single, it's often a huge challenge to face the end of the day alone, night after night.

Do you see the sin behind the sin in these instances? It's your unbelief in the face of whatever you find overwhelming. It's your response to the circumstance or situation causing fear, frustration, sadness, or stress that drives you to seek refuge someplace other than God. Our idolatry is always a turning away from God to embrace something else—some other source of comfort, security, or pleasure. In our despair, we turn to a false deliverer.

However, there's reason for encouragement when we begin to make the connections between the challenges of life in a fallen world and our sinful responses. We realize our sin isn't happening in a vacuum. There are increasingly predictable patterns to the places of unbelief, which are unique to each of us. If you haven't begun to see these patterns, you will. And when you do, it begins to change the face of the battle. When you're tempted, you begin praying about the sin behind the sin. You're no longer focused on pleading with God to make the desire to masturbate go away; you're pouring out your heart because of your loneliness—perhaps asking God for a spouse, but also confessing your anger that you don't yet have one. Instead of trying to fight going online, you're praying about the big project at work that's overwhelming you. Do you see how this transforms the battle? We begin to go deeper with God—and one another. As we do so, we learn that there's a snowball effect to righteousness—just as there is to sin.

One single man laughed with me as this truth became clearer. He had been free from porn for a number of months, but discovered that now at 9 p.m. each night, he began eating everything in his apartment. He had replaced porn with potato chips and ice cream. He had found a new idol to cope with his loneliness, but now that he realized it, he was ready to get back into the fight.

Until we begin to see the sin behind the sin, we stay stuck in patterns of behavior that seem impossible to break. This is the difference between focusing on what Tim Keller calls "surface idols" and "deeper idols."[26] Once we identify and develop accountability for the sin behind the sin, we are able to run to Christ sooner, and address those idols that are even more deeply entrenched than our struggle with sexual sin.

For Reflection:

1. What specific behaviors do you need to put off? What's your greatest area of weakness? Which behaviors continue to be an issue?

2. Where are the vulnerable places in your life? Which circumstances tend to be times of regular temptation and/or failure?

3. Do you understand the idea of sin behind the sin? What specific sources of stress, frustration, disappointment, loneliness, etc., provide an excuse to turn to sexual sin?

DAY 5: THE BATTLE PLAN

Finally, accountability should include a battle plan to address your current areas of weakness. If you're repeatedly struggling on your commute, you might need daily accountability—a quick call when you're leaving and another when you get home. We need to humble ourselves and ask for help. We need brothers to come to our houses and lock down the Internet and cable TV. Wherever you're struggling, you need to come up with a plan—with your brothers—how to overcome.

We also need battle plans when we're facing unique challenges. For example, prior to my wife's passing, I committed to her that when I traveled alone I wouldn't turn on the TV in the hotel room. This way I couldn't deceive myself that watching the news is harmless, then set myself up to start channel-surfing once it was over. One friend goes even further. Whenever he checks into a hotel, he tells the person at the front desk that they need to send someone up to his room to physically remove the TV. Maintenance guys across the country hate to see him coming, but he has a battle plan and is being ruthlessly violent with his sin.

You might have already noticed a pattern here: An important part of a battle plan is building fences, putting barriers around your sin. The goal is to draw the line in the sand before you act out on your sin of choice. It's like building a wall around a well, or a parapet on a roof. It's helpful to establish these seemingly obvious boundary lines when we're sane, because once we're in the throes of temptation all rational thinking goes out the window. In doing so, we give the Holy Spirit plenty of time to work on our conscience when we start crashing through these established roadblocks.

If you're channel-surfing on a business trip, chances are that even if you're not intending to seek out porn, part of you wonders if you might "accidentally" stumble across something. When you do, you need a lot of willpower in that moment to change the channel. You seem to be standing on firm ground, only to realize in an instant that you're on the edge of a precipice that is crumbling beneath your feet. But if you set up a barrier around TV on business trips, you're taking the high ground on the battlefield. Temptation still comes, the battle isn't any less intense, but you see the enemy coming. You're not caught in a guerilla ambush.

The intent of building these fences is to enable your conscience to kick in sooner. Crossing the line no longer happens when you view something inappropriate—it happens when you turn on the TV. Before you can even flirt with the idea of "innocently" channel-surfing, your heart is reined in. Roadblocks slow you down before you plummet over the edge. If you choose to break through this barrier, the Spirit will convict your conscience about the commitment you've violated, giving you further opportunity to turn back. It's true that if we're determined to sin, no safeguard is foolproof, but that's no reason not to make every effort on the front end to put up deterrents and invite repentance.

Does this sound legalistic to you? Nothing could be further from the truth. Legalism is an attempt to obey the law, to make it doable, so I can prove my worthiness before God. It seeks to establish a personal record of righteousness, rather than resting in the finished work of Jesus (see Romans 3:21–26 and Galatians 2:15–21). What we're talking about here is radically different. The whole point of building fences is based on the fact that I *know* I'm not righteous and that, given the chance, I'll act out. Far from attempting to establish righteousness, we need boundaries to keep our wayward hearts in check.

It's crucial, therefore, to consider your particular places of stumbling and take the necessary steps to safeguard your soul. If the Internet is a problem, putting accountability software in place is a bare-minimum necessity. Likely you need to take greater steps—using only a computer located in a prominent place in your home, committing to staying off the web when you're home alone, having the Internet password protected so you can go online only when someone else signs you in. You may need to block off certain streets, or even entire sections of the city. As discussed in Week 11, we need to be committed to radical amputation. You won't overcome your struggle with sexual sin unless you're committed to burning every bridge back to your folly. Our command, from Day 3, is to "put on the Lord Jesus Christ, and make no provision for the flesh." We need to be active in building fences so we make "no provision."

Here's the bottom line: it is hard to put on Christ and really revel in our relationship with him, as long as we continue to feed our flesh. If you keep eating slop at the world's trough, you'll have no appetite for the feast spread by your Father. Ultimate change comes as we learn, with Paul, "the surpassing worth of knowing Christ Jesus my Lord" (Philippians 3:8). Paul was willing to lose everything for Christ and declared that all his former boasts were dung compared to his relationship with Jesus. This is the only place we find contentment, joy, and rest for our souls. In order to get there, we have to let go of all our other false hopes. We must be willing to pass through the wilderness before we get to the Promised Land.

And a battle plan is only as good as the first engagement on the field. You need to constantly reassess and determine its effectiveness. Hint: If you're stumbling repeatedly, the battle plan isn't working!

For Reflection:

1. Where do you need to establish a battle plan? What are the specific situations where you regularly fail? What can you do to start addressing those issues?

2. How does considering the sin behind the sin affect your battle plan? Pray over those areas, talking to God about your fears, doubts, unbelief, anger, etc. How are these issues deeper than your struggle with lust?

3. What specific steps can you take to put on Christ, when confronted with temptation? Where do you most need to grow in your relationship with him?

WEEK 14:
CULTIVATING HUMILITY

KEY CONCEPT: All of us struggle with pride. It is humanity's underlying bent when we're living separated from God, but it continues to dog us even when we're in Christ. The Bible teaches that pride is our greatest enemy, and humility our closest friend. Pride leads us to covet and exploit others for our own pleasure. Since pride is the root of all sin, overcoming sexual sin requires us to be ruthless in battling pride.

God's sovereignty demonstrates the utter folly of our pride: We are dependent on him for everything. This is a place of profound spiritual warfare, because the enemy is desperate to poison us with pride. There is a grave danger when we grow self-righteous and judgmental, rather than reflect the humility and compassion of Jesus. The goal of the Christian life is to increasingly emulate Jesus and learn to trust the Father wholeheartedly, not leaning on our own understanding.

DAY 1: THE BIGGEST BATTLE

So many men are convinced that their struggle with lust is the biggest challenge they face, but by now you've realized that's not the case. Last week we observed that there's a lot more going on below the surface of our sin and that we need to uncover the sin behind the sin. But it gets worse.

The biggest battle we face, our fiercest enemy, is our own pride. John Stott said, "At every stage of our Christian development and in every sphere of our Christian discipleship, pride is the greatest enemy and humility our greatest friend."[27] In the last couple of weeks, we've looked at the importance of being merciless in the fight against our sin through Christ's power and the necessity of ruthless honesty if we're to overcome our struggle with sexual sin. But pride is, by far, the biggest hurdle.

To start with, sexual sin is bound up in pride. Our pride drives us to consume others, to be comfortable exploiting them for our own pleasure. Pride leads us to covet other men's wives or other men's bodies. When you think about it, coveting is really just pride as it relates to others. It is because we think so highly of ourselves that we decide, "They shouldn't have that—I should!" C. S. Lewis described pride "as essentially competitive—competitive by nature."[28] It is utterly committed to exalting self over others and, at the core, it is radically against God. Lewis added, "Pride leads to every other vice: it is the complete anti-God state of mind."[29]

C. J. Mahaney's definition is worth noting as well: "Pride is contending for supremacy with God and lifting up our hearts against Him."[30] As pride is the root of all sin, any hope of overcoming our sexual struggles requires us to engage in all-out war against our pride.

Of course, one of the great dangers about pride is that it's so hard to see. This is the ultimate place of self-deceit. We readily see it in others, but we're utterly blind to its presence in our own lives. And unlike so many other sins that are tied to our physical desires, pride is "purely spiritual: consequently it is far more subtle and deadly."[31] Paul warns against the pride that may result if a new convert is elevated to a place of spiritual authority, saying, "He must not be a recent convert, or he may become puffed up with conceit and fall into the condemnation of the devil" (1 Timothy 3:6).

Throughout Scripture, pride is linked to condemnation. Let's close today by considering the following sobering proverbs. Take some time to read them. Then read them again. Let them sink in, before moving on to the reflection questions:

> There are six things that the LORD hates,
>   seven that are an abomination to him:
> *haughty eyes*, a lying tongue,
>   and hands that shed innocent blood,
> *a heart that devises wicked plans*,
>   feet that make haste to run to evil,
> a false witness who breathes out lies,
>   *and one who sows discord among brothers*. (Proverbs 6:16–19,
>   emphasis added)

Everyone who is arrogant in heart is an abomination to the LORD; be assured, he will not go unpunished. (Proverbs 16:5)

Pride goes before destruction, and a haughty spirit before a fall. (Proverbs 16:18)

For Reflection:

1. How is pride "contending for supremacy with God"? How does it feel to know that it's an abomination to God?

2. How do you think pride is at work in your sexual sin? In what ways does it manifest itself?

3. Outside of sexual sin, where do you see pride in your life? Here are some tips: What do you base your image on? Who do you tend to look down on? By what criteria do you compare yourself to others?

DAY 2: THE FOLLY OF PRIDE

One of the crazy ironies of pride is that we actually have nothing to be proud of. From a biblical standpoint, everything has been given to us by God—our physical appearance, personalities, gifts and abilities, the family we were born into. In reality, we actually have control over very little. This is true for all of humanity, but it goes even deeper for those of us who struggle with sexual sin.

We are men who have been slaves to our appetites. When we're honest, we acknowledge that we're characterized by weakness and folly. We've been utterly confounded by our inability to stop doing things we don't want to keep doing. Yet when we begin to improve, we often grow proud. We actually begin to pat ourselves on the back because we no longer masturbate daily (or multiple times a day), that we haven't picked up a prostitute recently, that we've been staying away from the rest areas. What does that *say* about us?

C. S. Lewis describes the devil's glee over this state of affairs: "He is perfectly content to you becoming chaste and brave and self-controlled provided, all the time, he is setting up in you the Dictatorship of Pride—just as he would be quite content to see your [blister] cured if he was allowed, in return, to give you cancer."[32] As we'll see in a moment, if we take pride in our modest gains against sin, we are not only incredibly foolish but in grave danger.

How do you respond when you have a fall? Do you spiral into depression? Or kick your good works into high gear? Our response after we sin is as crucial as our response to the initial temptation. Often our response exposes our pride on a deeper level. Think about it: We usually beat ourselves up over our sin. What's going on there? We hate to see how bad we truly are. We hate that we continue to fall. We want to be better than that. It's all pride, and God is ruthlessly committed to rooting it out of our souls. Part of the reason we get stuck in sexual sin, and it doesn't seem like God is responding to our prayers for deliverance, is that God really wants us to begin battling the more foundational problem of pride.

In Week 12, I mentioned that God isn't big on formulas—right before I gave you one. Well, I'm going to do it again. Here's the last formula I'm aware of: God promises that if we'll humble ourselves, he'll give us grace.

> But he gives more grace. Therefore it says, "God opposes the proud,
> but gives grace to the humble." Submit yourselves therefore to God.

Resist the devil, and he will flee from you. Draw near to God, and he will draw near to you. Cleanse your hands, you sinners, and purify your hearts, you double-minded. Be wretched and mourn and weep. Let your laughter be turned to mourning and your joy to gloom. Humble yourselves before the Lord, and he will exalt you. (James 4:6–10)

Likewise, you who are younger, be subject to the elders. Clothe yourselves, all of you, with humility toward one another, for "God opposes the proud but gives grace to the humble." Humble yourselves, therefore, under the mighty hand of God so that at the proper time he may exalt you, casting all your anxieties on him, because he cares for you. Be sober-minded; be watchful. Your adversary the devil prowls around like a roaring lion, seeking someone to devour. (1 Peter 5:5–8)

Both passages call us to humility, and in the same context warn against (or at least anticipate) the work of the enemy. Killing pride and cultivating humility is our greatest battle and the place where we'll find the fiercest spiritual resistance. These passages call us to soberly assess our weakness and sin, to see ourselves as we truly are. We're called to humble ourselves in submission to church authority. As we discussed about accountability last week, this submission to authority keeps us aware of the structure of the universe.

Further, both passages quote an Old Testament passage, which features a stern warning coupled with a wonderful promise: "God opposes the proud but gives grace to the humble" (see Proverbs 3:34). First, the warning: God opposes the proud. This is why it's so serious if we become proud because of our growth in self-control. Our pride invites God's wrath. Destruction comes because we have set ourselves up against him—this is the most perilous place in the universe. Conversely, if we humble ourselves, we invite God's blessing. That again is the formula: If you humble yourself, God will give you grace.

In the battle against sexual sin, you know you need more grace. You know you can't fight this battle alone. You've probably been saying for years that you need God's help to be victorious. God is saying, *this* is how you get that help. Humble yourself and he will lavish grace upon you.

For Reflection:

1. Have you compared yourself to others, specifically regarding sexual sin issues, in order to feel better about your own behavior? What has that looked like? Over whom do you tend to exalt yourself?

2. Are you sobered to consider the reality of spiritual warfare surrounding the issue of pride? How can that fact help you cultivate greater humility?

3. Consider your responses to failure. Since God opposes the proud, how might this issue have kept you stuck in sexual sin? Does it encourage you that more grace is freely offered to you? Why or why not?

DAY 3: THE POWER OF WEAKNESS

None of us wants to be weak. From a young age, we're told that the essence of manhood is our strength. And yet, as discussed in Week 7, our striving for independence runs completely counter to God's design for us.

But the need to embrace our weakness isn't just about our need for the body or the power of Christ. God calls us to embrace, in a much more profound way, the reality of our utter weakness and inability in order to receive the grace of God. Listen to Paul's experience:

> So to keep me from being too elated because of the surpassing greatness of the revelations, a thorn was given me in the flesh, a messenger of Satan to harass me, to keep me from being too elated. Three times I pleaded with the Lord about this, that it should leave me. But he said to me, "My grace is sufficient for you, for my power is made perfect in weakness." Therefore I will boast all the more gladly of my weaknesses, so that the power of Christ may rest upon me. For the sake of Christ, then, I am content with weaknesses, insults, hardships, persecutions, and calamities. For when I am weak, then I am strong. (2 Corinthians 12:7–10)

In Week 10 we looked at our need for Christ's power in us. Here Paul shows us how this dynamic works. Jesus meets us in our weakness. He knows the arrogance of our hearts, and in his severe mercy he brings us to our knees. Men have confessed their arrogance to me, acknowledging that they would never have become Christians if not for their struggles with same-sex attraction or porn addiction. Like Paul, God humbles us for our own good, to keep us from growing conceited.

In Week 9 we looked at Romans 8:28–29 and the reality that God's ultimate good for us is to be conformed to the image of Jesus. What does that mean? As the second Adam, Jesus came to live the life originally expected of all humanity. God's design for his creature, in the words of Andrew Murray, was "to present itself an empty vessel, in which God can dwell and manifest his power and goodness."[33] Instead, we chose to live for our own glory and have been trying to fill ourselves ever since. Lewis' description of pride's "essential competitiveness" is what happens when creatures destined for infinite, eternal glory believe they're left to fend for themselves in a finite world.

Jesus was so radically different. In the wonderful poem of the early church found in Philippians 2, he is described as not clinging to his status as God, but humbling himself to become human. We can't possibly begin to get our minds around that reality—what it meant for Jesus to set aside his power and glory, his infiniteness, to become an embryo. He became a servant, ultimately humbling himself to the most shameful and excruciating death imaginable. Consider him riding into Jerusalem on a donkey (not a war horse), weeping over the lost city as he comes. See him at the Last Supper removing his outer garment and washing his disciples' filthy feet.

Listen to Jesus' self-description and his invitation to us: "Come to me, all who labor and are heavy laden, and I will give you rest. Take my yoke upon you, and learn from me, for I am gentle and lowly in heart, and you will find rest for your souls. For my yoke is easy, and my burden is light" (Matthew 11:28–30).

Jesus is calling us to be yoked to him. This is an invitation to know and experience his strength, and yet he emphasizes his humility and gentleness. He calls us to know his humility and, through it, to experience his power. To be humble is to be truly human. It is returning to God's design for humanity, perfectly demonstrated for us in the life of Jesus.

For Reflection:

1. Aside from your struggle with sexual sin, what else has God brought into your life to humble you? Are there other ways he's calling you to see your weakness and receive his strength? Explain.

2. How has God used sexual sin to humble you? How do you see his love for you in that?

3. From your knowledge of the Gospels, describe the humility of Jesus. What blessings would there be in taking up Jesus' yoke and learning humility from him? What will it cost you?

DAY 4: MORE LIKE JESUS

It's astounding to consider Jesus' humility. When all the Jews were marveling at his teaching, blown away because he had no formal education, he answered, "My teaching is not mine, but his who sent me" (John 7:16). That one particularly strikes home with me because I like to say profound, spiritual things. I'm excited when someone is impacted by an insight I've *received* from Scripture. Sure, I can write the appropriate disclaimer, but in the moment I want all the credit.

Have you ever been ready to dash off and tell someone some spiritual truth because the insight made you look insightful? Jesus said things that blew people away, and yet he never took credit for his insight. He constantly demonstrated his divine power—healing the sick, calming storms with a word, raising the dead. But in all this, he was never puffed up, never showing off. He prayed for grace and gave the Father all the credit for the miracles that took place.

What does it look like to put on humility and become more like Jesus? Andrew Murray said, "Accept every humiliation, look upon every fellow-man who tries or vexes you, as a means of grace to humble you. Use every opportunity of humbling yourself before your fellow-men as a help to abide humble before God."[34] There are so many daily opportunities for us to humble ourselves—when a driver cuts you off, when someone shoves in line, when you're overlooked for a promotion, when your spouse treats you unfairly. Consider what Peter tells us of Jesus, from firsthand experience:

> For to this you have been called, because Christ also suffered for you, leaving you an example, so that you might follow in his steps. He committed no sin, neither was deceit found in his mouth. When he was reviled, he did not revile in return; when he suffered, he did not threaten, but continued entrusting himself to him who judges justly. He himself bore our sins in his body on the tree, that we might die to sin and live to righteousness. By his wounds you have been healed. For you were straying like sheep, but have now returned to the Shepherd and Overseer of your souls. (1 Peter 2:21–25)

How do you respond when you're sinned against? Have you ever noticed that Jesus is never defensive? He entrusted himself to the Father. This is so important for us because we're focused on *our* glory. Little children quickly learn the word *fair*. (That's considered an f-bomb in my house!) We're readily attuned to whether *we're* receiving the treatment we believe we deserve, but we tend to be pretty oblivious to the needs of others around us. Further, we're so ready to defend our own honor as soon as it's called into question. How do you respond when you're unjustly accused? Do you entrust yourself to the one who judges justly?

Marriage is a key area where this is a problem. Though not always the case, wives who have been burned by their husbands' sexual sin tend to struggle with trust. As a result, many husbands have wives who ask them a litany of questions any time they're five minutes late leaving the office or take an unexpected errand. How do you respond to this? Many men get angry. Particularly as you work hard on your marriage, it can feel really defeating. It seems like it doesn't matter what you do, you'll always be judged by the past.

But how you respond in these moments is crucial! In humility, can you see past her behavior to your sin that precipitated the "20 questions" routine? I challenge men that the sincerity of their repentance isn't demonstrated by the first dozen or so responses to questioning, but by how they respond to the 537th time they're grilled.

Of course, this assumes that a husband and wife will be jointly working on the marriage with others. It's *not* okay for wives to refuse to forgive and grow bitter over their husband's sin, not acknowledging his repentance and growth. But she needs other people in her life to point her to Christ—she's not going to be willing to hear from *you*!

There's such a tragic irony in this: Our sin has brought about our wives' insecurity, but we get angry when we're asked. And the problem of defensiveness isn't limited to marriage. It's ready to flare any time we're not walking in humility. Jobs have been lost, churches split, friendships severed, and families torn apart because people refused to humble themselves. In any conflict, someone must be willing to break the downward spiral of escalation, to humble himself and seek forgiveness and show mercy. Let that person be you.

For Reflection:

1. Who in your life is most vexing on a regular basis? What would it look like for you to go out of your way to show kindness and love to this person?

2. Where are you suffering injustice? How might God be using this to humble you? At what point is it okay to fight back? Explain your answer.

3. How are you responding to your wife's lack of trust? Are you tired of hearing about your sin and just want her to get over it already? Where do you need to be more humble in your marriage?

DAY 5: WOLVES IN SHEEP'S CLOTHING

Not all that masquerades as Christian lines up with the Bible and points us to Christ. Be wary of anything "Christian" that doesn't cultivate humility. If it creates pride and self-righteousness, run like the wind! Listen to C. S. Lewis again, "How is it that people who are quite obviously eaten up with Pride can say they believe in God and appear to themselves very religious? I am afraid it means they are worshipping an imaginary God."[35]

In this passage, Lewis suggests that perhaps these good religious people are those Jesus had in mind when he told of those on the last day who will come saying, "Lord, Lord . . . " only to hear Jesus' horrific reply, "I never knew you" (see Matthew 7:21-23). Because pride is such a crucial enemy of our soul, we need to be ruthless in rooting it out—even when it comes in acceptable Christian garb.

Obviously, there are extreme examples: "Christians" who picket the funerals of gays and lesbians, glorying in their condemnation and grievously sinning against family and friends in mourning. Many of us have strong political opinions on both sides of the aisle, and we look down on members of the opposing party with scorn. As we explored in Week 5, there's a push to remake Jesus in our image, celebrating aspects of maleness that do not promote humility in the least. But here's the interesting thing: When Jesus was asked by the disciples who would be the greatest in the kingdom, he didn't rebuke them for the question. He just radically redefined what "greatness" is all about:[36]

> And Jesus called them to him and said to them, "You know that those who are considered rulers of the Gentiles lord it over them, and their great ones exercise authority over them. But it shall not be so among you. But whoever would be great among you must be your servant, and whoever would be first among you must be slave of all. For even the Son of Man came not to be served but to serve, and to give his life as a ransom for many." (Mark 10:42–45)

Jesus calls us to walk this road with him—a road starkly different than the path that brought us to this point. He invites us to leave behind our selfish exploitation of others, to relinquish the demand that sex bring life, to be set free from the tyranny of our pride. He isn't calling us to a boring, meaningless existence, but to one that overflows with life, even as the battle rages around us. He invites us to enter his rest, even as we must continue in our labors. He has promised his faithfulness to us—that he will complete the work he's begun in us.

Are you ready to venture forth with Christ and your brothers?

Consider this call to walk in humble dependence on God, moment by moment through your days. Jesus promises that as you do, you'll experience refreshment and healing. He is faithful, and he will do it!

Trust in the LORD with all your heart, and do not lean on your own understanding. In all your ways acknowledge him, and he will make straight your paths. Be not wise in your own eyes; fear the LORD, and turn away from evil. It will be healing to your flesh and refreshment to your bones. (Proverbs 3:5–8)

ENDNOTES

Introduction

1. When Jesus was challenged by the Sadducees about the resurrection, he countered that there would be no marriage in heaven (see Matthew 22:23–33; Mark 12:18–27; Luke 20:27–40).

2. See Genesis 25:29–34 and Hebrews 12:16–17.

Week 2

3. For a fuller discussion, see Harry Schaumburg, *False Intimacy* (Colorado Springs: NavPress, 1997).

4. C. S. Lewis, *The Weight of Glory and Other Addresses* (New York: Harper Collins, 1980), 26.

Week 3

5. An extremely insightful book on the devil's strategies in our lives is C. S. Lewis's *The Screwtape Letters* (San Francisco: HarperOne, 2001).

Week 4

6. This is the Hebrew name for God, rendered in most English translations as "Lord."

7. N. T. Wright, *The Climax of the Covenant* (Minneapolis: Fortress Press, 1993), 141.

Week 5

8. For a helpful critique of the masculine Jesus men's movement, see Brandon O'Brien, "A Jesus for Real Men," *Christianity Today*, April 18, 2008. http://www.ctlibrary.com/ct/2008/april/27.48.html accessed August 11, 2010

9. Quoted in O'Brien, "A Jesus for Real Men."

10. Samson's sexual weakness with Delilah is well known, but did you know that his first wife was the result of lust in rebellion against God's command (Judges 14:1–3) and that he spent time with prostitutes (Judges 16:1)?

Week 7

11. Bob Dylan, "Gotta Serve Somebody," from the album *Slow Train Coming*, 1979.

12. C. S. Lewis, *Mere Christianity* (New York: HarperCollins, 2001), 134.

13. Andrew Bonar, ed., *Letters of Samuel Rutherford* (Carlisle, PA: Banner of Truth Trust 1984), 400.

Week 8

14. Dave Harvey, "God, My Heart, and Stuff," in *Worldliness: Resisting the Seduction of a Fallen World*, ed. C. J. Mahaney (Wheaton: Crossway, 2008), 103–4.

Week 9

15. John F. Kennedy, Inaugural Address, January 20, 1961, www.bartleby.com. (Accessed December 5, 2011.)

Week 11

16. John Eldredge, *Wild at Heart: Discovering the Secret of a Man's Soul* (Nashville: Thomas Nelson, 2001), 184.

17. Bruce Marshall, *The World, The Flesh, and Father Smith* (Boston: Houghton Mifflin, 1945), 108.

18. Bonar, 290.

19. C. S. Lewis, *The Problem of Pain* (New York: The Macmillan Company, 1962), 56.

20. *The Westminster Confession of Faith*, VIII.II in *The Westminster Standards* (Suwanee, GA: Great Commission Publications, 2001), 11.

Week 12

21. I am indebted to Ed Welch for this insightful contrast in his book *Addictions: A Banquet in the Grave: Finding Hope in the Power of the Gospel* (Philipsburg, NJ: P&R Publishing Company, 2001), 181–84.

22. Lewis, *The Weight of Glory*, 38.

Week 13

23. Jerry Bridges, *Discipline of Grace: God's Role and Our Role in the Pursuit of Holiness* (Colorado Springs: NavPress, 1994), 116–17.

24. Erich Maria Remarque, *All Quiet on the Western Front* (New York: Fawcett Crest, 1957), 100.

25. Oswald Chambers, *If You Will Ask: Reflections on the Power of Prayer* (Grand Rapids: Discovery House Publishers, 1989), 13.

26. For an extremely helpful book on this topic, see Timothy Keller, *Counterfeit Gods: The Empty Promises of Money, Sex and Power and the Only Hope that Matters* (New York: Dutton, 2009).

Week 14

27. Quoted in C. J. Mahaney, *Humility: True Greatness* (Colorado Springs: Multnomah, 2005), 29.

28. C. S. Lewis, *Mere Christianity*, 122.

29. Ibid.

30. Mahaney, *Humility*, 31.

31. Lewis, 125.

32. Ibid.

33. Andrew Murray, *Humility & Absolute Surrender* (Peabody, MA: Hendrickson, 2005), 6.

34. Ibid., 47.

35. Lewis, *Mere Christianity*, 124.

36. I am indebted to Mahaney for this insight, *Humility*, 43.